Intermediate ESL Lesson Plans

A Conversational Approach

STUDENT READER
STUDENT WORKBOOK
TEACHER GUIDE

**Includes
The History of Flight Lessons
with full audio**

Learning English Curriculum

Since 1999

www.efl-esl.com

Daisy A. Stocker B.Ed., M.Ed.
George A. Stocker D.D.S

Learning English Curriculum

Copyright © 2023 ALL RIGHTS RESERVED.

You are permitted to print or photocopy as many copies as you need for your school. Online distribution is not permitted. Please contact us if you wish to teach online.

Re-Sales is not permitted.

Notice: Learning English Curriculum makes every reasonable effort to obtain from reliable sources accurate, complete, and timely information about the tests covered in this book. Nevertheless, changes can be made in the tests or the administration of the tests at any time and Learning English Curriculum makes no representation or warranty, either expressed or implied as to the accuracy, timeliness, or completeness of the information contained in this book. Learning English Curriculum make no representations or warranties of any kind, express or implied, about the completeness, accuracy, reliability, suitability or availability with respect to the information contained in this document for any purpose. Any reliance you place on such information is therefore strictly at your own risk.

The author(s) shall not be liable for any loss incurred as a consequence of the use and application, directly or indirectly, of any information presented in this work. Sold with the understanding, the author is not engaged in rendering professional services or advice. If advice or expert assistance is required, the services of a competent professional should be sought.

Published by:
Learning English Curriculum

ISBN 9781772454253

Visit us on the Web at
https://www.efl-esl.com

Licensing
Licensing is a white label service, (our name does not appear) which allows your organization to edit, modify, the curriculum to suit your needs.
https://efl-esl.com/license-our-esl-curriculum/

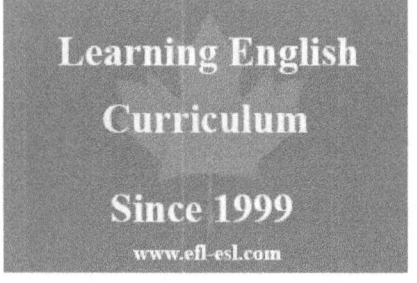

Learning English Curriculum
Victoria, B.C. Canada
E-mail: **info@efl-esl.com**

About Learning English Curriculum Ltd.

Learning English Curriculum began in Czechoslovakia in 1990. Shortly after the Velvet Revolution that freed the country of Communism. The authors began writing these lessons as they taught English to their Czech Students at the English Centre in Karlovy Vary. The students played a vital role in the development of this series. The authors consulted with them by having them complete student surveys wherein they rated the extensive variety of activities and lessons that they had participated in. Discussion of the results followed and any item that was rated below 8, on a scale of 1 to 10, was discarded. Thus, Learning English Curriculum evolved through consultation with our English second language students.

Since 20095 thousands of people around the world have visited our web sites. At this time purchases of our Teen-Adult Curriculum, Children's Curriculum, Children's Storybooks and our listening programs have been made from more than 100 countries.

At Learning English Curriculum, we have a suggestion regarding the printing of our books in an economical and environmentally friendly way. It is our experience that when students begin something new there are always those that, for a number of reasons, don't continue. In order to cut expenses and avoid wasting paper, we suggest that you begin the classes by providing only the first lessons of the printed book. These small things do make a difference.

Customization of your covers

You may be interested in the customization of your covers. (White Label Services
This personalizes your textbooks and makes them a visible part of your school's curriculum. For this service contact us at: info@efl-esl.com

Members of our team with professional degrees have combined years of teaching experience and editing to produce these teaching materials.

Team Members for this publication:

Daisy A. Stocker B.Ed., .Ed.
Dr. George A. Stocker D.D.S.
Brian Stocker MA

CONTENTS

Lesson 1	An Opportunity or a Problem	1
Lesson 2	Living in a New Place, the Future Progressive tense	3
Lesson 3	Finding Interesting Groups of Friends, Use of "going to"	5
Lesson 4	Solving Problems, Review and Test	7
Lesson 5	A Young Girl Finds Her Way	9
Lesson 6	Lady Gaga, Count and Non-count Nouns	10
Lesson 7	Electric Cars, Subject and Object Pronouns	13
Lesson 8	Electric Cars Continued and Test	16
Lesson 9	Aliens!	18
Lesson 10	Never Give Up!	20
Lesson 11	Gospel Music	22
Lesson 12	Review and Test	25
Lesson 13	The British Royal Family – Queen Victoria	26
Lesson 14	The British Royal Family – Edward VII	28
Lesson 15	Edward VIII Falling in Love	30
Lesson 16	The Hero King and Test	32
Lesson 17	Charles Prince of Wales	33
Lesson 18	Princess Diana of England	36
Lesson 19	Diana, Princess of Broken Hearts	38
Lesson 20	The Monarchy Must Survive, Final Test	39

Intermediate ESL Lesson Plans

A Conversational Approach

Student Reader

LESSON 1

VOCABULARY:
relocate (to)	active (to be)	twice	bore (to)
advantage	disadvantage	gas	opportunity
commute (to)	whether	unhappy [not happy]	village
depart (to)	manage (to)	kid (slang for a young person)	drama

ACTIVITY 1:

Listen to your teacher read each paragraph. Then take turns reading the sentences orally.

AN OPPORTUNITY OR A PROBLEM

Alex is unhappy because his work in an insurance office is boring. He has an offer of a better job as manager of a small office in a village fifty kilometers away. He will be paid more, but his family must decide whether they want to relocate.

His teenage children are in high school. They are athletic and enjoy playing on many teams. His wife, Martha, has job a teaching pre-teen students in a middle school. She enjoys it and she is also very active with a music group in their church. Her music group meets twice a week.

ACTIVITY 2:

Divide into small groups. Ask and answer the questions orally, then check your answers with those supplied in the box.

1. What kind of office does Alex work in? 2. Why is Alex unhappy? 3. What will he do in the small village? 4. How far away is the village? 5. Why is the small office job better? 6. What must his family decide? 7. What kind of school do his teenage children attend? 8. What do his children enjoy doing? 9. What does Martha do at work? 10. How old are pre-teen students? 11. Is Martha musical? 12. How often does Martha's music group meet? 13. Martha is "very active" with a music group. 14. What does that mean?	1. He works in an insurance office. 2. He is unhappy because his office work is boring. 3. He will manage a small office. 4. The village is fifty kilometers away. 5. It's better because he will be paid more money. It will be more interesting. 6. They must decide whether they want to relocate. 7. They attend high school. 8. They enjoy playing on many sports teams. 9. She teaches pre-teen students. 10. They are ten, eleven or twelve years old. 11. Yes, she is musical. 12. It meets twice a week. 13. It means that she does a lot of work with them.

EXERCISES 1 AND 2 – WORKBOOK PAGE 1
EXERCISE 3 – WORKBOOK PAGE 2

Student Reader

LESSON 1 CONTINUED

ACTIVITY 3: **WHOLE CLASS ACTIVITY**

BRAINSTORM: **WHAT SHOULD ALEX DO?** List everyone's ideas on the board.

The students then move about the room asking: **What do you think Alex should do?** When they find others who agree with them, they are to sit down together and decide why they made that decision. They are then ready to tell the class what they decided and why.

ORAL QUESTIONS **TEACHER'S GUIDE**

ACTIVITY 4 – WORKBOOK PAGE 2

EXERCISE 4 – WORKBOOK PAGE 2

ACTIVITY 5: Listen to your teacher read the dialogue. Role-play it for the whole class. Then divide into small groups and role-play it several times, changing roles each time.

NARRATOR: Alex and Martha are talking about moving to the small village.

ALEX: My job here is really boring. I need a change.

MARTHA: I understand how you feel but I like my job and my music group.

ALEX: It would be expensive for me to commute because the price of gas is so high.

MARTHA: Can you ask for another job here in the city?

ALEX: Yes, but it would be the same as the one I have. In the village I'll be the manager.

MARTHA: I worry about moving our family. Our kids would miss their friends and the sports.

ALEX: That's true, but I don't know what to do.

MARTHA: Perhaps you should commute. The price of gas may go down.

ALEX: The company would pay me more, so I'd have more money for transportation.

MARTHA: I think that's the best plan. Let's tell the kids that we aren't going to move. They'll be happy about that and I feel okay about it too.

ALEX: Alex goes to tell his kids about his decision.

NARRATOR: Hi, everyone. We've decided to stay here. We aren't going to move. I'll commute.

ALEX: KIDS: That's cool, Dad. Thanks!

ACTIVITY 6 – WORKBOOK PAGE 3

ACTIVITY 7 – WORKBOOK PAGES 3 AND 4

Student Reader

LESSON 2

VOCABULARY:	that suits me = I like	might as well = why don't	full-time
volleybal	that shoot (to)	we? hunter	farmer
I nothing	pond	reply (to)	bargain (to)
duck	look forward to (to)	how much	spare time
part-time	expenses	literature	wonder (to)

LIVING IN A NEW PLACE   ACTIVITY 1:
Listen to your teacher read the paragraphs. Then take turns reading the sentences aloud.

Sarah and Peter moved to Vancouver a few months ago. They work part-time to pay for their expenses at college. They don't have much spare time or money for other activities. They are both interested in sports, music and literature and would like to meet others with the same interests.

Sarah is meeting new friends from her history class. Tonight, Peter is joining some people from work for a volleyball game. As they talk about their evening, he is wondering where they can meet new friends.

THE FUTURE PROGRESSIVE TENSE
This tense is used to talk about something that will be in progress sometime in the future.

In Beginners lessons you studied the present progressive tense.
The present progressive tense uses <u>the verb "to be" plus the present participle</u>:
The present participle ends in "ing". I am visiting my aunt.
The future progressive tense, uses the verb "to be"+ the present participle in the future tense.
<u>I will be visiting</u> my aunt tomorrow.
<u>They will be having</u> lunch at 12 o'clock tomorrow.

ACTIVITY 2:   Listen to your teacher read the dialogue.
The bold faced words show the use of the future progressive tense.

SARAH: What **will you be doing** after work tomorrow, Peter?

PETER: I am hoping to play volleyball instead of studying. Are you planning something?

SARAH: There's a concert at the theater. I talked to Marie and Anne in history class yesterday.

PETER: They **will be going** and I thought I might go too.

SARAH: Good idea. I guess **I'll be getting** home around nine o'clock.

PETER: Okay. The concert **will be finishing** at about that time.

SARAH: Will you need the car?

PETER: **I'll be meeting** Marie and Anne on the bus so I won't need the car.

SARAH: Well, I might as well take the car to work. Then we can start playing earlier.

PETER: Let's plan to have supper after we get home.

SARAH: That suits me – **I'll be looking forward** to it!

ACTIVITY 3: Divide into small groups and role-play the dialogue, changing roles several times. **EXERCISE 1 – WORKBOOK PAGE 5**

Student Reader

LESSON 2 CONTINUED

ACTIVITY 4: Ask and answer these questions. Then check your answers.

1. What will Peter be doing after work tomorrow?
2. What will Sarah be doing?
3. Will Sarah be going to the concert with Peter?
4. Who will Sarah be meeting?
5. Who will be taking the car?
6. When will they eat supper?
7. What will Peter be looking forward to?
8. What is Peter wondering about as they tal about their evening?

1. He will be playing volleyball.
2. She will be going to a concert.
3. No, she won't be going to the concert with Peter.
4. She'll be meeting Marie and Anne.
5. Peter will be taking the car.
6. They'll eat supper after they get home.
7. He'll be looking forward to his supper.
8. He's wondering where they can meet new friends.

EXERCISE 2 – WORKBOOK PAGE 5

ACTIVITY 5: Divide into groups of two or three. Ask each other these questions and answer in sentences using the future progressive tense. (will be + the present participle)

1. Do you know what you will be doing tomorrow?
2. Will you be playing volleyball tomorrow?
3. Will you be taking the bus to work in the morning?
4. Will you be going to a concert tonight?
5. Will you be getting married next week?
6. Will you be going to the movies tonight?
7. Will your friend be visiting you this weekend?
8. Will you be going to town tomorrow?
9. Will you be buying a dog next week?
10. Will you be eating dinner at home tonight?

ORAL QUESTIONS   TEACHER'S GUIDE

ACTIVITY 6: Listen to your teacher read this joke.

A hunter was returning home with nothing in his bag when he saw some ducks swimming in a little pond. An old Scottish farmer was watching them.
"How much do you want to let me shoot those ducks?" asked the hunter.
"Half a dollar," was the reply. The hunter shot, killing fourteen ducks.
"Well," said the hunter, smiling as he paid the farmer, "I guess I got the best of that bargain."
"Ah, I don't know," replied the Scotchman.
"They're not my ducks – and it's not my pond."

EXERCISES 3 AND 4 – WORKBOOK PAGE 6

LESSON 3

VOCABULARY:

college	own	same as	semester	information
row (to)	kayak (to)	what about	club	awful
limerick	rather	offer (to)		

ACTIVITY 1:   **FINDING INTERESTING GROUPS**
Listen to your teacher read this paragraph. Then take turns reading the sentences orally.

When Peter and Sarah talked to some of the students at the college, they found that many of them came from another city or country. They, too, wanted to find other friends. They wanted to belong to groups of people with interests the same as their own.

THE FUTURE PROGRESSIVE TENSE ALSO USES:

TO BE + GOING TO + BE + THE PRESENT PARTICIPLE

NOTE: "be going to" is used to talk about something that will happen in the future.
It is making a prediction.
Sarah and Peter are talking about what they **are going to be doing** next semester.

ACTIVITY 2:   Listen to your teacher read the dialogue. Divide into small groups and practice role-playing. Then role-play it for the whole class.

NARRATOR: Sarah and Peter are talking about what they **are going to be doing** next

SARAH: semester. I'd like to find out about where we can meet new people – do new things.

PETER: How are we going to get some information?

SARAH: Where can we look?

PETER: I'd sure like to join a group interested in water sports.

SARAH: I'd like to try rowing.

PETER: So would I, or perhaps kayaking.

SARAH: We could look in the phone book, or what about the YM-YWCA?

PETER: Let's phone the Y and see what they **are going to be offering** during the next

SARAH: semester. It would be great if we could go on a Saturday for a few hours.

NARRATOR: Peter phones the Y. The girl who answers tells him that soon they **are going to be printing** their brochure for the next semester. He gives them his address.

PETER: They **are going to be printing** their brochure for next semester. They'll sent it to us in a couple of weeks.

SARAH: Did you ask if they**'re going to be including** water sports?

PETER: She said they'd have a number of groups for swimming, rowing and kayaking.

EXERCISES 1 AND 2– WORKBOOK PAGE 7

Student Reader

LESSON 3 CONTINUED

ACTIVITY 3: Divide into small groups. Ask and answer the questions. Check the answers in the box.

1. How many semesters does your school have each year?
2. Are you going to be moving soon?
3. What are you going to be studying next semester?
4. Is your school going to be having a rowing team?
5. What group would you be interested in joining?
6. Are you going to be joining the YM-YWCA?
7. Are you going to be including English in your studies next semester?
8. What interesting activity are you going to be doing next semester?
9. Would you look in the phone book if you wanted to join a group?
10. Would you need to find friends if you moved to a different city?

---

1. My (Our) school has ____ semesters each year.
No, I'm not going to be joining the YM- YWCA.
2. Yes, I'm going to be moving soon.
No, I'm not going to be moving soon.
my studies next year.
3. I'm going to be studying ____ next semester.
4. Yes, my (our) school is going to be having a rowing team.
No, my (our) school isn't going to be having a rowing team.
5. I'd be interested in joining _____.

6. Yes, I'm going to be joining the YM- YWCA.
7. Yes, I'm going to be including English in
8. I'm going to be …
9. Yes, I'd look in a phone book if I wanted to join a group.
10. Yes, I'd need to find friends if I moved to a different city.

ORAL QUESTIONS ACTIVITY 4:

TEACHER'S GUIDE

Listen to your teacher read this

limerick.

A LIMERICK
I'd rather have fingers than toes; I'd rather have ears than a nose; And as for my hair,
I'm glad it's all there.
I'll be awfully sad when it goes.

EXERCISES 3 AND 4 – WORKBOOK PAGES 8 AND

9 ACTIVITY 5 – GUIDE PAGES 13 AND 14

Student Reader

LESSON 4   REVIEW

VOCABULARY:	knife	fork	foreign
solve (to)	get used to (to)	manners	lonely
			either

ACTIVITY 1:   SOLVING PROBLEMS

Alex, Martha, Sarah and Peter all had problems to solve. **Alex** had a good job offer but he had to think about his family, too. **Martha** needed to be able to visit her parents. **Sarah and Peter** were new to the city. They wanted to make new friends and to meet people with interests that were the same as their own.

What did they do to solve their problems?
Brainstorm with your whole class your understanding of what they did to solve their problems. Write your ideas on the board and match each solution to a problem that it might solve.

ACTIVITY 2: Divide into groups of two or three. Ask and answer these questions. Then check your answers with those in the box.

1. Are you going to be joining a new group next semester?
2. Are you going to be getting your hair cut tomorrow?
3. Where are you going to be going tonight?
4. Are you going to be eating at noon tomorrow?
5. Are you going to be looking for a better job soon?
6. Are you going to be talking to your family next week?
7. Are you going to be sleeping in tomorrow?
8. Are you going to be solving a problem tonight?

1. Yes, I'm going to be joining a new group next semester.
   No, I'm not going to be joining a new group next semester.
2. Yes, I'm going to be getting my hair cut tomorrow.
   No, I'm not going to be getting my hair cut tomorrow.
3. I'm going to be going …
4. Yes, I'm going to be eating at noon tomorrow.
   No, I'm not going to be eating at noon tomorrow.
5. Yes, I'm going to be looking for a better job soon.
   No, I'm not going to be looking for a better job soon.
6. Yes, I'm going to be talking to my family next week.
   No, I'm not going to be talking to my family next week.
7. Yes, I'm going to be sleeping in tomorrow.
   No, I'm not going to be sleeping in tomorrow.
8. Yes, I'm going to be solving a problem tonight.
   No, I'm not going to be solving a problem tonight.

ORORAL QUESTIONS
TEACHER'S GUIDE

EXERCISES 1 AND 2
WORKBOOK PAGE 10

Student Reader

LESSON 4 CONTINUED

ACTIVITY 3: Divide into small groups and role-play this dialogue several times.

NARRATOR: Carmen and Ming have both arrived in a foreign country. They have left their home countries to study English.

CARMEN: I just arrived here two months ago.

MING: I came during the summer.

CARMEN: Did your family come with you?

MING: No, I'm alone.

CARMEN: My family isn't going to be coming either. I want to learn English and then return to my country.

MING: I'll be able to get a good job back home if I know English.

CARMEN: It's the same for me. I'm lonely. I sure miss my friends.

MING: Me too, and the place where I live is so different to home.

CARMEN: What about the food? It'd be wonderful to have some of Mom's home

MING: cooking! I can't get used to their manners – saying please and thank

CARMEN: you all the time. Yes, and I can't get used to the way everyone uses their knife and fork.

MING: I hope to make some good friends here, but I need friends who speak English, too.

CARMEN: We'd better get back to class. They'll be starting soon.

MING: Let's go.

ACTIVITY 4: Return to the large group - brainstorm the difficulties that you are having as you study English and list them on the board. Your difficulties might be like Ming's and Carmen's or they might be about learning English. Study your list and identify the most common problems.

ACTIVITY 5 - WORKBOOK PAGE 11   GUIDE PAGES 16 TO 19

Student Reader

LESSON 5

VOCABULARY:

overweight	born	fit in (to)	perform (to)	gain (to)
admission	study (to)	social issues	politics	contract
forward	eccentric	shape (to)	famous	album

ACTIVITY 1: Listen to your teacher read the paragraphs, then take turns reading the sentences.

A YOUNG GIRL FINDS HER WAY

In 1986, a young girl, Stefani Germanotta was born. When she went to school, the other girls didn't like her: she was overweight, she was thought to have a big nose, and really didn't "fit in". She learned to play the piano at age 4, and by age 14, was performing in bars and at parties.

At 17, she gained admission to New York University's Tisch School of Music. At university, she studied song writing, art, religion, social issues and politics. This life did not suit her, though. At age 19, she left university, started her own band, and moved out of her parent's home.

She signed a contract with Def Jam Records, in 2006, but unfortunately it came to nothing. Bitterly disappointed, she moved back home. Here she thought about the way forward, experimenting with eccentric clothing, drugs, and dancing in bars.

She worked as a song writer for a time, and in 2008, released her first album "The Fame".

These difficult years shaped the thinking, and career of the famous lady who became Lady Gaga.

ACTIVITY 2: Divide into small groups. Ask and answer the questions. Then check your answers.

1. Where was Lady Gaga born?
2. Was she interested in music?
3. Why did she leave university?
4. When did she learn to play the piano?
5. Do you think that the difficult years helped her find her way?

---

1. She was born in New York City.
2. Yes, she was interested in music.
3. University life didn't suit her.
4. She learned to play the piano at age 4.
5. Yes, I think the difficult years helped her to find her way.

EXERCISES 1 and 2 – WORKBOOK PAGE 12

ORAL QUESTIONS TEACHER'S GUIDE

ACTIVITY 3 – WORKBOOK PAGE 12,
   GUIDE PAGES 25, 26

ACTIVITY 4 – BINGO - WORKBOOK PAGE 13

Student Reader

LESSON 6

VOCABULARY:

album	popular	celebrity	perform (to)	critical
strange	extreme	costume	proud	release (to)
empower (to)	community	compassion	acceptance	love (to)
important	famous	message	compassion	bravery
glamorous	luxury	inauguration	discrimination	

ACTIVITY 1: Listen to the teacher read the paragraphs. Then take turns reading the sentences.

LADY GAGA

In 2008, Lady Gaga released her first album "The Fame". This was followed in 2009 by her first big hit "Just Dance". The girl, Stefani, who was not popular at school, suddenly became a celebrity: Lady Gaga. Her music was very popular. In 2009 she wrote and performed in "The Fame Monster", which received many awards.

At this time, many people were critical of her strange and extreme fashions. When questioned about pictures of her in bizarre costumes, she said: "Be yourself and love who you are and be proud. Because you were born this way, baby."

In 2011, her album "Born This Way" was released, followed by a hugely successful world tour. During the tour, she often gave speeches, telling her fans "to be whoever you want to be". Her success was accompanied by a great deal of criticism because its message empowered women as well as the gay community. Her answer was that her mother taught her "acceptance, tolerance, bravery, and compassion." The people loved her.

Although she made many millions of dollars, she said that this was not important to her, she said she wanted a glamorous life, not a life of luxury.

In 2020 President elect Joe Biden asked her to sing the National Album at his inauguration. Perhaps this was the greatest honor of all.

" Don't you ever let a soul in the world tell you that you can't be exactly who you are."

ACTIVITY 2: Role-play the dialogue below.

NARRATOR: Role-play the conversation below:

Francis: Lady Gaga is certainly very different!
Nancy: She likes to wear crazy clothes and make-up.
Bill: I think she uses these things to send a message to people.
Francis: What kind of message, Bill?
Bill: She is trying to tell the world that it is alright to be different.
Nancy: Maybe you're right, Bill! There is so much discrimination in the world.
Francis: Yes, I think you're right, Bill. She is telling people to turn away when people judge you, and be yourself.
Nancy: That's a good kind of message!

Student Reader

LESSON 6 CONTINUED

COUNT AND NON-COUNT NOUNS

A COUNT NOUN is one that can be made plural. These items can be counted.

EXAMPLES: desks   books   chairs   lights   pencils   women   men   girls   boys   offices

"Many" with count nouns.
I saw many **elephants**.   I didn't see many **elephants**.   I saw an **elephant**.

NON-COUNT NOUNS cannot be counted. They have no plural form.

EXAMPLES: music   coffee   sunlight   furniture   slang
progress   knowledge   advice   homework   information

Much with non-count nouns.
Does he have much **energy**?   Does he have much **energy**?

Yes, he has a lot of **energy**.   He doesn't have much **energy**.

Student Reader

LESSON 6 CONTINUED

USING MUCH WITH NON-COUNT NOUNS Much is often used in negative sentences and questions.

    QUESTION: Do the students have **much** homework?
    NEGATIVE ANSWER: No, the students don't have **much** homework.

MUCH IS **NOT** USED IN A POSITIVE SENTENCE.
USE: A LOT / A LOT OF
    POSITIVE ANSWER: Yes, the students have **a lot of** homework.

USING **A LOT OF** WITH NON-COUNT NOUNS
A lot / a lot of can be used with any question or answer, positive or negative. It is always correct to use **a lot** or **a lot of** with count or non-count nouns.

    EXAMPLES:
Do you like to listen to a lot of music?
Yes, I like to listen to a lot of music.
No, I don't like to listen to a lot of music.
Yes, I like music a lot.
    NOTE EXCEPTIONS:
Much can be used in a positive sentence with an adjective, adverb, or preposition.
    EXAMPLE:
Much of the furniture is new.
I did **so much** homework last night that I was tired.
I liked the music **very much**.
I ate **too much** dinner. I ate **much more** than you did.

ORAL QUESTIONS   TEACHER'S GUIDE

ACTIVITY 3: Divide into small groups and read the text below. Then answer the questions orally.

A group of English students are practicing their English outside the classroom. They won't have much time, because the class starts in fifteen minutes. Bill and Nancy had to work, so they came later than the others. They didn't have much time to practice their English. They hardly had time for supper, and Bill said that he would need much more supper after class.

1. Will the students have much time before class?
2. Why did Bill and Nancy come later than the others?
3. Did Bill and Nancy have much time for supper?
4. What was Bill going to do after class.
5. Do you have much time to practice English?

EXERCISE 1, 2, and 3 – WORKBOOK PAGE 14

ACTIVITY 4 – WORKBOOK PAGE 15

EXERCISE 4 – WORKBOOK PAGE 16

ACTIVITY 5 TEACHER'S GUIDE PAGES 29 and 30

Student Reader

LESSON 7

VOCABULARY:	government	replace (to)	driverless
scene	transportation	steam engine	popular
status	wealthy	change gears	one third
symbol	mass produce	factory	common
smell (to)	(to) steam	miles per hour	forget (to)
vehicle			

ACTIVITY 1: Listen to your teacher read the paragraphs, then take turns reading the sentences.

ACTIVITY 1: Listen to your teacher read the paragraph, then take turns reading it aloud. Although scenes like the one above may still be common in some parts of the world, people have always looked for better, faster, quieter, and cleaner forms of transportation.

In 1769, a German invented the "Dampfwagen". This was a car with a steam engine.
It took almost an hour to make enough steam to move, and its water supply soon ran out, unless it was refilled.

From 1896 to 1930, there were more than 1500 companies making cars in the United States. The first electric vehicle was made in 1890, with a top speed of 14 miles per hour. In the early part of the 20th century, for a short time, the electric car was very popular. It became a status symbol for the wealthy people in society. It was quiet, did not need the driver to shift gears,
and it was easy to start. Because it was easy to start and to drive, ladies could drive a car for the first time.
Although we think electric cars are very modern, the idea is very old. Between 1900 and 1912, one third of all the cars on the road were electric cars. They were much easier to drive, there was very little noise, and you didn't have to change gears.

Student Reader

LESSON 7 CONTINUED

In 1908, a man called Oliver Fritchle opened a factory that could make 198 cars a year by 1912.
When Henry Ford started making his Model T cars in 1908, his new factories could sell these cars for $650.00. The Fritchle electric cars cost almost three times that amount.

So, after a wonderful start, the electric cars were forgotten, and gas powered cars became popular.

ORAL QUESTIONS   TEACHER'S GUIDE
ACTIVITY 2:   **Role-play the following dialogue.**

NARRATOR: Sarah and Peter are talking about electric cars.

SARAH: I thought that electric cars were something new!

PETER: That's what I thought, too but they were making them more than 100 years ago!

SARAH: Henry Ford used a new idea in his factory. Each worker did just one thing as the car moved slowly past them.

PETER: I think that his cars were much cheaper than electric cars, so the cars with gas engines became the most popular.

SARAH: Yes, I read that you could buy a new Ford for about $650.00, while electric cars cost almost three times that amount.

PETER: I wonder what kind of cars we will be driving in another 100 years?

SARAH: Well, I think they will be very different from today's cars!

Student Reader

LESSON 7 CONTINUED

SUBJECT AND OBJECT PRONOUNS

The pronouns below are the **subject** of the statement. (Subject pronouns)

I / **you** / saw an electric car.
He / she / it / was hungry.
One feels hungry in the morning.
We / **you** / **they** / saw a picture of an electric car.

The following pronouns are the object of the statement. (Object pronouns)
They can be used with or without a preposition. Example: He worked **for them**. They helped **us**.

EXAMPLES:
Our friend Peter has an electric car. He showed it to **me**.

Later, he drove to our house and showed it to **us**.
Did he show his new car to **you**?
He is very happy when he drives **it**.

I saw **him** yesterday. Electric cars are great! I'm going to get **one**!

EXERCISES 1 AND 2 – WORKBOOK PAGE 17

EXERCISES 3 AND 4 – WORKBOOK PAGE 18

ACTIVITY 3: Divide into groups of 3 or 4. Read the paragraph and answer the questions.

Electric cars were very popular more than 100 years ago. In the early 1900's, about one third of all cars on the road were electric cars. They were much easier to drive, there was less noise, and they did not smell bad. At the same time, Henry Ford built huge factories that mass produced cars with gas engines. Because the Ford cars were so much cheaper, people soon stopped buying electric cars.

1. Why did people like electric cars so much?

2. Why were the early gas engine cars so difficult to drive?

3. If you buy an electric car now, many governments are giving out money to help pay for the car. Why are they doing this?

4. Will electric cars soon become more popular that gas engine cars?

5. If electric cars replace cars with gas engines, what will this do to the oil and gas industry?

Student Reader

LESSON 8

ACTIVITY 1: **WHOLE CLASS ACTIVITY**

Listen to your teacher read the paragraph below. Then take turns reading the sentences. Take turns answering the questions orally.

"The future of the auto industry is electric. There's no turning back."
In the spring of 2021, President Joe Biden said these words after testing the Ford 150 light electric truck at its testing site. His government is investing $174 billion to help this new industry get started. The Ford 150 light truck is one of the most popular vehicles on the road, and now it has brought out an all-electric model.

There are signs of this change everywhere: A company called Rivian has been hiring 150 people a week to work in its factories. They have an order from Amazon for 100,000 light electric trucks.

Many cities in North America are replacing all of their municipal vehicles with electric vehicles. At the same time, many of the bus companies in these cities are replacing their buses with electric buses. In this way, they save a great deal of money on fuel and maintenance, and stop polluting the air.

1. Do you think President Biden was right when he said: **"The future of the auto industry is electric?"**

2. What does **"There is no turning back"** mean?

3. Is the American government going to help the auto industry change to making electric cars?

4. Why are bus companies switching to electric buses?

5. Do you think the high price of gas will make people think about buying an electric vehicle?

ACTIVITY 2: **Divide into small groups. Ask each other the questions. Answer in sentences, then check your answers.**

1. Why are governments spending money to help the auto industry to switch to making electric cars?	*1. Governments want to stop the air pollution from gas engines.*
2. If you were buying a car today, would you buy an electric car?	*2. Yes, I would. No, I wouldn't.*
3. Do you think it's important to be concerned about air pollution from gas engines?	*3. Yes, I think it's very important.*

ORAL QUESTIONS   TEACHER'S GUIDE

Student Reader

LESSON 8 CONTINUED

ACTIVITY 3:
Divide into groups of three or four.
Think about the changes in society in the future when all of the vehicles are electric. Discuss the following questions.
Report to the whole class.

1. What would cars be like if the first Ford cars weren't so successful?

2. Will driverless trucks be used a lot in the future?

3. Already, new cars have safety features, for example, they will stop automatically, if there is something in the way. Do you think driverless cars will be safer that present day gas cars?

4. President Biden said: "The future of the auto industry is electric. There's no turning back." Do you think electric vehicles will replace all the gas engine vehicles in the future?

5. Will the change to electric vehicles be a good change for society?

6. Many, many delivery trucks are making short runs to deliver goods in the cities. Why are electric vehicles well suited to this work?

Two electric driverless trucks that are planned for the future.

EXERCISE 1 AND 2 – WORKBOOK PAGE

19 ACTIVITY 4 – WORKBOOK PAGE 20

EXERCISE 3 – WORKBOOK PAGE 21

Student Reader

LESSON 9

VOCABULARY:

creature
community
send (to)
speed bright
planet
TV station
strange
space
flash (to)
crazy
officer
machine
pilot (to)
wake up (to)
flying saucer
rocket ship |
alien
broadcast (to)
enough

ACTIVITY 1: Listen to your teacher read the paragraphs. Then take turns reading the sentences aloud.

ALIENS!

Did you ever see an alien? They are creatures that come from other planets. They arrive in strange machines that can fly at the speed of light. Their flying ships are many shapes – some are like the rockets that we send into space and others are shaped like saucers.

There are often stories in the newspapers or magazines about people who have seen these spaceships and the aliens that pilot them. It's hard to believe the stories that

You are living in a community where a spaceship full of strange aliens has just landed. Strange things are happening! You can't believe what has happened to you!!

The police don't believe what they are hearing. The television, radio and newspaper reporters are very excited because everyone will listen to their broadcasts and buy their newspapers. Some people are very frightened. They are phoning the newspapers, television stations and radio stations. No one knows what to do.

EXERCISES 1 AND 2 – WORKBOOK PAGE 22

Student Reader

LESSON 9 CONTINUED

ACTIVITY 2:
Divide into small groups. Ask and answer these questions. Then check your answers.

1. What planet do we live on?
2. Name some other planets that go around our sun.
3. How do the aliens in this story travel?
4. How fast can their flying ships go?
5. Why would the newspapers be happy if some aliens arrived?
6. Why would you want to meet an alien?
7. Why would you want aliens to stay on their own planet?
8. Do you believe that aliens will come from other planets?
9. Would you believe the television if they showed a picture of an alien?
10. How would you feel if you met an alien?
11. What would your friends think if you said that you saw one?
12. If you met an alien, what would you do?
13. What do you think an alien would look like?

---

1. We live on Earth.

2. The other planets are: Mercury, Venus, Mars, Jupiter, Saturn, Uranus, Neptune and Pluto.

3. They travel in a spaceship.

4. They can go at the speed of light.

5. They would have exciting news and sell a lot of papers.

6. I'd want to see what it looked like.
   I'd want to hear it.
   I'd want to see what it would do.

7. They could be dangerous.
   Our planet is crowded.
   They could make us sick.

---

8. Yes, I believe they will come.
   No, I don't believe they will come.

9. Maybe, but I'd want to know more.
   No, they could make the pictures.

10. I'd be excited.
    I'd be frightened.
    I'd feel great. Everyone would know me.

11. They'd think I was crazy.

12. I'd try to talk to it.
    I'd call the police.
    I'd run as fast as I could. I'd invite it to a party.

13. It wouldn't look like me! It would have...

ACTIVITY 3 – TEACHER'S GUIDE PAGES 38 AND

39 EXERCISES 3 AND 4 – WORKBOOK PAGE 23

Student Reader

LESSON 10

VOCABULARY	fans	stuff	aloud
stands working out pitch (to) reach (to)	tramp come back (to) suddenly	make good (to) win (to) forget (to)	warm-up(to) injure (to) bill had been

Phrases to understand:
  my arm may come back. – my arm may get better
  pay it back any time – pay something back when you can
  get out there – join the others
  the stands buzzed – the people in the stands talked
  ninth inning – the ninth time that the two teams had changed places from **at bat** to **out in the field**
  a ground ball – a ball that hits the ground near the home plate and doesn't go far.
  to strike out – the batter misses the ball three times

ACTIVITY 1:   Listen to your teacher read this famous baseball story on Pages 20 and 21.
Then take turns reading the sentences aloud.
Next, role-play the first page of the story with the whole class.
Take turns being the narrator, McGraw, Jack Scott

NEVER GIVE UP!

It was a July morning. In New York, the Giants baseball players were working out under their manager, John McGraw. A man who looked like a tramp walked slowly up to McGraw.

"Well?" said McGraw. "What do you want?"

"I am Jack Scott," the man answered.

Once Jack Scott had been a fine pitcher. Now he had a bad arm.

"Hello, Scott," said McGraw. "How are you?"

Scott looked unhappy. Nobody in baseball wanted him any longer. He hadn't been a successful farmer. When his farm buildings had burned down he had lost everything. Now he and his wife and son were living in town. They had one cheap little room.

"Mr. McGraw," he said, "they say you always give a ball player a second chance. Will you let me work out with your club? My arm may come back."

McGraw reached into his pocket.
He put a fifty-dollar bill into Scott's hand.

"Pay it back any time," he said.
"Be here tomorrow. Bring your stuff."

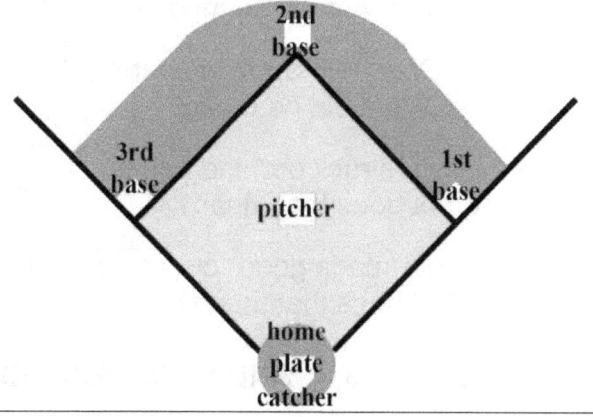

Student Reader

LESSON 10 CONTINUED

THREE MONTHS LATER

Three months later, a game was about to begin. 50,000 excited fans sat in the stands. They came to see the third game of the World Series. It was between the Giants and the Yankees.

Suddenly McGraw said, "Get out there, Scott, and warm up! You're pitching today!"

When the crowd heard Scott's name, the stands buzzed. Was McGraw going to start this baseball tramp against the Yankees?

At first the crowd buzzed as Scott pitched. However, nobody will ever forget that game. In the ninth inning the Giants were leading 3 to 0.

Babe Ruth, a famous player for the Yankees, walked to the plate.
He went out on a ground ball. Scott struck out the next batter. Two out and Bob Meusel was at bat. The wind-up, the pitch, and Meusel hit a grounder. It was an easy third out.

The game was over. Jack Scott made good on his second chance by winning a World Series for the Giants and for kind hearted John McGraw.

ACTIVITY 2:
Whole class activity. Brainstorm your answers and write them on the board.

1. How did Jack Scott feel as he walked up to McGraw?
2. What kind of a person was McGraw?
3. How do you think Jack Scott felt as he started to pitch the ball?
4. Why do you think kindness might help people who have difficulties?

ACTIVITY 3: Divide into groups. Ask and answer these questions.

1. The Giants were "working out". What does that mean?
2. How does a tramp look?
3. What is a bad arm?
4. Did Scott have a lot of money?
5. What is a "second chance"?
6. McGraw said, "Bring your stuff." What did he mean?
7. McGraw told Scott to "warm up" What did he mean?
8. Scott "struck out" the batter. What does that mean?
9. Scott "made good" on his second chance. What does that mean?

---

1. They were practicing.
2. A tramp looks unhappy and is likely wearing very old clothes.
3. A bad arm is an injured arm.
4. No, he didn't have much money.
5. It lets someone try again.
6. He meant that Scott should bring his things for playing baseball.
7. Warming up means to get your body moving.
8. Scott pitched balls that were too fast and difficult for the batter to hit.
9. It means that he worked hard and succeeded.

ORAL QUESTIONS TEACHER'S GUIDE

EXERCISES 1, 2, 3, 4, AND 5 – WORKBOOK PAGES 24 AND 25

Student Reader

LESSON 11

VOCABULARY:			
spirituals [religious songs]	pianist	jazz	blues
gospel music	experience (to)	pregnant	asleep
weak	precious	storm	Lord
funeral	worn out	desolate	combine (to)
piano	skill	military	patriotism

GOSPEL MUSIC

ACTIVITY 1: Listen to your teacher read the paragraphs. Then take turns reading the sentences orally.

Long ago in the United States, Blacks heard a lot of music in church. They combined this music with their own sad blues, adding to them, and finding their own way to sing them.

Later, the pianist, composer and singer, Thomas Dorsey put their spirituals, jazz and blues together to make "Gospel Music".

Then, one day he had a terrible experience that changed his life. He had to play at a church meeting. He went early in the morning, leaving his pregnant wife asleep. He left quietly, thinking happily about their expected child. While he was away, his wife and baby died.

Feeling desolate and lost, Dorsey went to the music room of his old school and started playing the piano. He said that the words and the music he started writing:

> "Precious Lord, take my hand, lead me on, let me stand. I'm tired, I'm weak, I'm worn, through the storm, through the night, lead me to the light. Take my hand, precious Lord, lead me home."

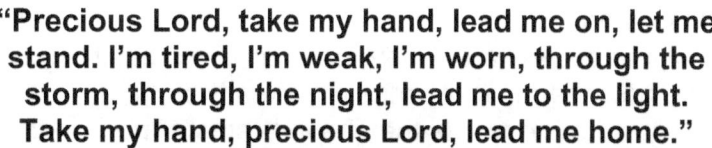

In his darkest hours, Dorsey composed the greatest gospel song ever written. Mahalia Jackson, who sang nothing but gospel music, sang this song at Martin Luther King's funeral.

EXERCISES 1 AND 2 – WORKBOOK PAGE 26

Student Reader

LESSON 11 CONTINUED

ACTIVITY 2: Divide into small groups. Ask and answer these questions orally. Then check your answers with the answers in the box.

1. Where did Blacks hear a lot of music?	1. They heard a lot of music in church.
2. What did they combine with their own songs?	2. They combined the church music with their own songs.
3. What did Dorsey combine to make Gospel Music?	3. He combined Blacks spirituals, jazz and blues to make Gospel Music.
4. What changed Dorsey's life?	4. The death of his wife and baby.
5. How did Dorsey feel as he went to the music room of his old school?	5. He felt desolate and lost.
6. What did Dorsey do when he felt so sad?	6. He played the piano.
7. Do you know this gospel song?	7. Yes, I know it. No, I don't know it.
8. Where was this gospel song sung?	8. It was sung at Martin Luther King's funeral.

ACTIVITY 3:
Write these kinds of music on the board leaving space for the students to add some words under each one.

Popular	Jazz	Temple Music	Religious
Gospel	Rap	Country and	Music
Rock	Patriotic music	Western Dance music	Classical

Each student is to choose their favorite kind of music from the list.
Then they are to move about the room asking the other students:
What is your favorite kind of music?
When they find others who like the same kind of music they are to move about the class together looking for others to join them. If someone likes music that no one else enjoys, they are to choose again
and join a group.

Small Groups
When all the groups are ready, each group is to sit together and brainstorm words that describe how their favorite music makes them feel.
Then they write the words they have brainstormed on the board under the name of their favorite music.

Large Group Discussion
Each student is to look for something that they **don't agree with** and tell the class:

- why they don't agree
- how that kind of music makes them feel

Student Reader

LESSON 11 CONTINUED

ACTIVITY 4:
Divide into small groups. Ask and answer these questions. Then check your answers with those in the box.

1. Does a pianist play the piano?
2. Are there many churches in our country?
3. Do you play the piano?
4. Are musicians sometimes actors or actresses?
5. Are some songs religious?
6. Do you know some gospel songs?
7. Does jazz make you feel good?

> 1. Yes, a pianist plays the piano.
> 2. Yes, there are many churches in my country. No, there aren't many churches in my country.
> 3. Yes, I play the piano. No, I don't play the piano.
> 4. Yes, musicians are sometimes actor or actresses.
> 5. Yes, many songs are religious.
> 6. Yes, I know some gospel songs. No, I don't know any gospel songs.
> 7. Yes, jazz makes me feel good. No, jazz doesn't make me feel good. I haven't ever heard any jazz.

EXERCISE 3 - WORKBOOK PAGE 27

ACTIVITY 5: Listen to your teacher read this, then take turns role-playing:

Two Canadian girls talk about music
Basma and Lia are classmates. Basma came to Canada two years ago, to escape the civil war in Syria. Lia's parents came from China when she was a baby. They are talking about music.
Basma: In Syria, there was never any Western music, it is all new and different to me.
Lia: I think in China they are hearing a lot of Western music now. Likely the older people still prefer the traditional Chinese music.
Basma: I really like the music that came out after the second war. They Had big bands. Tommy Dorsey, Duke Ellington and Glenn Miller played some wonderful music, that is still popular today.
Lia: That's very different to the electronic music that we hear today! Instead of a big band, there is one person, working on a computer. I think I prefer the music that comes from a live band.

ACTIVITY 6 – WORKBOOK PAGE 27

ACTIVITY 7: Divide into small groups
The military uses music to inspire bravery and patriotism in its soldiers. Movie makers use music to set the mood in their movies. All the religions use music to send a message to the people. Advertisers use music to sell their products. Some students like to listen to music while they study, other people like to listen to music while they work. Almost every society on earth uses music to dance to and to celebrate.

Each group should decide what kinds of music they like, when they like to listen to music, and how they like to use music. Make a list, and be prepared to share it with the whole class.

ORAL QUESTIONS   TEACHER'S GUIDE

Student Reader

LESSON 12 REVIEW

> **VOCABULARY:**
> scenario   sell (to)   Classical   Popular   Rock   Guitar   perhaps

ACTIVITY 1: Listen to your teacher read about these people's problems.

The people didn't know what to do about the green men that took their things.

Jack Scott used to be a famous baseball pitcher but he had to stop pitching because of his injured arm.

When Thomas Dorsey was very sad, he wrote a religious song.

Whole Class Activity
Write the answers to these questions on the board. What was your best solution for the green men?
How did Jack Scott solve his problem?

What was your best solution for Ethan?

Discuss these questions:

1. Is there one solution for all the problems?

2. Could the people who met the green men, Jack Scott, or Thomas Dorsey learn from any of the others? If "Yes" what could they learn?

3. Think about this scenario:
   Martin will lose his job if he doesn't learn English.
   He attended some English classes but he didn't do well because he was sick. Should he give up?

Brainstorm what he should do? Think about some of your other solutions. Perhaps those ideas will help you to help him.

Write your ideas on the board. Then decide which one is the best. You may want to combine several to get the best solution.

ACTIVITY 3 – WORKBOOK PAGE 28

EXERCISES 1 AND 2 – WORKBOOK PAGES 29

ACTIVITY 3 – WORKBOOK PAGE 30

ORAL QUESTIONS   TEACHER'S GUIDE

Student Reader

LESSON 13

VOCABULARY:	get up (to) [to get out of bed]		
influence	moral	century	social
(to) set (to)	queen	touch (to)	cover (to)
pretend (to)	necessary	reject (to)	illegitimate
poor	suffer (to)	poverty	code

ACTIVITY 1: Listen to your teacher read the paragraphs, then take turns reading the sentences.

THE BRITISH ROYAL FAMILY - QUEEN VICTORIA

The British Royal Family influenced the moral code of the British people for centuries. They were the social leaders, setting the example for social behavior.

When Victoria became queen in 1838, she changed the moral code of the people. Men were to be at home with their families each evening. A man could kiss a woman's hand but he shouldn't touch her. Only married couples should touch each other. Women were to wear clothes that covered them from their shoulders to their ankles. Some things were not to be talked about.

Queen Victoria also influenced the moral code of the people in the countries that were a part of the British Empire. Although some of these people followed the queen's example, many of them just pretended.

There were many disadvantages. Families and society rejected unmarried women who had babies. Only the poorest kind of work would be available to them and to their children. If a woman couldn't marry before the birth of her child, she was sure to live in poverty for the rest of her life. The rich solved the problem of illegitimate children with money, but most women suffered a life of poverty.

ACTIVITY 2: Work in small groups. Ask and answer the questions. Then check your answers.

1. What did the British Royal family influence?
2. Where were the men to be each evening?
3. Where could a man kiss a woman?
4. Did everyone follow the queen's moral code?
5. What happened to women with illegitimate babies?
6. Did illegitimate children have problems?

---

1. They influenced the moral code of the Empire.
2. They were to be at home.
3. He could kiss her hand.
4. No, many people just pretended.
5. They were rejected by their families and society.
6. Yes, they had many problems.

Student Reader

LESSON 13 CONTINUED

**WORDS THAT SHOW OPPOSITION
THEY EXPRESS OPPOSITE IDEAS**

whereas   but   on the other hand

EXAMPLES:
Queen Victoria set a moral code, **but** many people didn't follow it. She thought she was right **whereas** they thought she was wrong. The rich had no problems. **On the other hand,** the poor suffered.

ACTIVITY 3:
Divide into groups of three or four.
Each group is to make three sentences that express opposite ideas. Write them in your notebooks and be ready to read them to the class. Use **whereas**, **but,** and **on the other hand.**

ACTIVITY 4:
Divide into groups of three or four and ask each other these questions. Then check your answers.

1. Would you want to live here now, or in Britain during Queen Victoria's time?

2. Could you agree with Queen Victoria?

3. If women's clothes covered them from their shoulders to their ankles, would they be comfortable?

4. Could you solve more of your problems if you were rich?

5. Who has the greatest influence in this country?

6. Do most people stay at home in the evening?

7. Do you think the Queen of England could influence the moral code of the British people today?

8. The rich could use their money to help with some problems. Do you think that this made them happy?

---

1. I'd want to live during Queen Victoria's time.
   I'd want to live here now.
2. Yes, I could agree with Queen Victoria.
   No, I couldn't agree with Queen Victoria.
3. Yes, they'd be comfortable.
   No, they wouldn't be comfortable.
4. Yes, I could solve more of my problems if I were rich.
   No, I couldn't solve any more of my problems.
5. _____ has the greatest influence.
6. Yes, most people stay at home in the evening.
   No, most people don't stay at home.
7. Yes, I think she could.
   No, I don't think she could.
8. Yes, I think it did.
   No, I don't think it did.

EXERCISES 3, 4 AND 5 – WORKBOOK PAGE 32   **ORAL QUESTIONS TEACHER'S GUIDE**

EXERCISES 6 – WORKBOOK PAGE 33   **EXERCISES 1 AND 2 – WORKBOOK PAGE 31**

Student Reader

LESSON 14

VOCABULARY:

well known	plenty	age	depression
power	throughout	vote (to)	crown (to)
control	in spite of	spend (to)	suffragette

ACTIVITY 1:
Listen to your teacher read the paragraphs, then take turns reading the sentences.

THE BRITISH ROYAL FAMILY - EDWARD THE VII

THE AGE OF MEN

Edward VII, the oldest son of Queen Victoria, was crowned king in 1902 at the age of 60. Before becoming king, he and his wife traveled throughout Europe, attending the theaters and enjoying the friendship of all the other royal families

When he was crowned at the beginning of the twentieth century he was well known and well liked in both Britain and Europe. In spite of the coming war, it was a time of good living, parties, dances and beautiful clothes for the rich.

There were songs to sing, there was plenty to drink and the men had control of their world. The British Empire was at
 its strongest, it was the "Age of Men". The rich men had the power until Edward died in 1910, nothing could stop them, not even the suffragettes who wanted to be able to vote.

Then the difficult times came. First the war, then the depression, and finally another war.

EXERCISES 1 AND 2 – WORKBOOK PAGE 34 EXERCISES 3 AND 4 – WORKBOOK PAGE 35

Student Reader

LESSON 14 CONTINUED

ORAL QUESTIONS   TEACHER'S GUIDE
ACTIVITY 2:
Divide into groups of two or three. Ask each other these questions. Answer in sentences. Then check your answers.

1. Would you want our country to have a king?
2. Would you want to spend your life waiting to be king?
3. Would you get bored if you were visiting friends all the time?
4. When you know there will soon be a war, is it a good idea to have as much fun as you can?
5. Is today the "Age of Men" in this country?
6. Do the rich people have most of the power in our country?
7. Do you think that kings and queens worry about the poor people?
8. Did our country suffer during the 1930's?
9. Are there plenty of theaters near here?
10. Are you well known in this city?
11. Do poor people often suffer?

---

1. Yes, I'd want our country to have a king.
   No, I wouldn't want our country to have a king.
2. Yes, I'd want to spend my life waiting to be king.
   No, I wouldn't want to spend my life waiting to be king.
3. Yes, I'd get bored if I were visiting friends all the time.
   No, I wouldn't get bored if I were visiting friends.
4. Yes, it's a good idea to have as much fun as you can.
   No, it isn't a good idea to have as much fun as you can.
5. Yes, I think it's the "Age of Men".
   No, I don't think it's the "Age of Men".
6. Yes, the rich people have most of the power.
   No, the rich people don't have most of the power.
7. Yes, I think that kings and queens worry about poor people.
   No, I don't think that kings and queens worry about poor people.
8. Yes, our country suffered during the thirties.
   No, our country didn't suffer during the thirties.
9. Yes, there are plenty of theaters near here.
   No, there aren't many theaters near here.
10. Yes, I'm well known in this city.
    No, I'm not well known in this city.
11. Yes, poor people often suffer.

ACTIVITY 3: Divide into groups of two or three. Choose a scenario and role-play it for the class.

SCENARIO 1: You are a married couple. You live in England in 1903. Your husband just learned that you are a suffragette! He is angry. You want to vote.

SCENARIO 2: It is 1904 in England. You are two ladies. You are walking along the street looking in the shop windows when a woman asks you for some money, because she is very hungry.

SCENARIO 3: You are a group of men sitting in your club. It is in London in 1903. You are talking about Queen Victoria's wish that men stay home in the evenings. You say that the new King Edward doesn't ever stay at home. One of the men says that this is the "Age of Men", and you should be able to stay out every night.

EXERCISE 5 – WORKBOOK PAGE 36

LESSON 15

VOCABULARY:

divorce (to)	true	fall in love (to)	violin
reflexive	mall	heart's desire	forgive (to)
give up (to)	throne	government	pardon (to)
empire	pub	upper class	alone

ACTIVITY 1: Listen to each of the paragraphs and answer the questions in sentences.

THE BRITISH ROYAL FAMILY
EDWARD THE VIII FALLING IN LOVE

In 1936 King George V died and his son Edward VIII became king. At the age of 42, he was a party loving man with little interest in government. After less than a year as king, he fell in love with a divorced American woman. Edward was in love! He must marry the woman he loved and Wallis Warfield Simpson was his true love.

Nothing could stop him, not even an Empire!

Although the people loved this good-time king, they said "No" to this marriage. Could the queen of England be a divorced American? The answer was "Never!" Could they accept a divorced woman as queen? A divorced woman could never be queen! An American could never be their queen!

Then, as the people of the Empire watched, Edward gave up his throne for the woman he loved. Then he left for France where he married his heart's desire, Wallis Warfield Simpson. His younger brother George became king, but to the day he died in the 90's, the British Royal Family never forgave him.

ACTIVITY 2:

Divide into groups of two or three and role-play the dialogue several times.

NARRATOR: Edward and Wallis are in Buckingham Palace.

EDWARD: At last, we are here

WALLIS: together. It's nice to be

EDWARD: Will you marry me?

WALLIS: How can we marry? The people will never accept me.

EDWARD: They love me. I'll tell them of my great love for you. They'll understand.

WALLIS: Oh Edward! What about your family?

EDWARD: We'll find a way.

ACTIVITY 3 – WORKBOOK PAGE 38
EXERCISE 1, 2 AND 3 – WORKBOOK PAGE 37

Student Reader

LESSON 15 CONTINUED
ORAL QUESTIONS   TEACHER'S GUIDE

ACTIVITY 4:   Divide into groups of two or three. One student reads the sentence. The next student repeats the sentence adding one of these adverbs.

mostly	**seldom**	**frequently**	**never**	**generally**
always	**hardly ever**	**occasionally**	**often**	

1. The queen goes to London.
2. The British people love their royalty.
3. A lot of tourists go to Buckingham Palace.
4. The queen cooks dinner.
5. The Royal Family sets an example.
6. Edward VIII went to parties.
7. The queen visits other countries.
8. The royal family forgave Edward.
9. Queen Victoria wore long dresses.
10. King Edward VII danced in spite of the shadows of war.
11. Edward VIII loved Wallis Warfield Simpson.
12. Queen Victoria liked to run.

REFLEXIVE PRONOUNS
A reflexive pronoun usually refers to the subject of a sentence.

EXAMPLE: **She** looked at **herself** in the mirror.

Used with "by" a reflexive pronoun usually means "alone".

The **boy** wrote the letter **by himself**.

myself	ourselves
yourself	yourselves
himself, herself, itself	themselves

ACTIVITY 5:   Stay in your groups and practice adding a reflexive pronoun to each sentence.

1. The girl walked home.
2. The boy wrote the best paragraph.
3. You must solve the problem.
4. We really need to study.
5. They cleaned the room.
6. The dog was at home.

ACTIVITY 6:   Divide into small groups.
Brainstorm the advantages and disadvantages of Edward VIII marrying Wallis Warfield Simpson. Each group is to decide the advantages and disadvantages, then report to the class.

The advantages and disadvantages should be written on the board as the groups report.

Whole class discussion: "Was Edward right to give up the throne to marry Wallis Simpson? The whole class votes.
ACTIVITY 7 – WORKBOOK PAGES 38, 39, 40, AND GUIDE PAGES 54, 55 AND 56

Student Reader

LESSON 16

THE HERO KING

VOCABULARY				
monarch shy	famous	courage	divorce	throne
comfort (to)	stammer	inspire (to)	bomb (to)	speech therapist
	injured	hospital	survivor	example

Although he never expected to be king, and didn't want to be King, King George VI was one of the best loved monarchs England ever had. During the war, his famous speeches on the radio gave the British people the courage to continue the fight against the German enemy. After his father, George V died, George's brother Edward became king. Edward was in love with Wallace Simpson, a divorced American woman. By British law, the king could not marry a divorced woman, so Edward gave up his right to the throne.

George was a very shy man, and he had a terrible stammer. Sometimes his stammer was so bad, he could hardly speak. Now, as King, he would be expected to give wonderful speeches to inspire his people.

King George worked very hard with a speech therapist, and he overcame his speech problems.

Three years after becoming king, the Second World War started. King George, along with Winston Churchill, spoke to the people frequently on the radio, and helped the people to keep up their courage during the terrible days of the war.

King George and Queen Elizabeth stayed in Buckingham Palace, even though it was bombed nine times by German war planes. When London was bombed, King George and Queen Elizabeth immediately visited the area and tried to comfort the people. They were often seen visiting the injured in the hospitals, and comforting the survivors.

King George and Queen Elizabeth became an example for people all over the world.

ACTIVITY 1:
Divide into groups of three or four.
Write five sentences in your notebooks that describe why you think King George VI was heroic. Each group should read their sentences to the class.

ORAL QUESTIONS   TEACHER'S GUIDE

**EXERCISES 1,2 and 3 – WORKBOOK PAGE
41 EXERCISE 4 – WORKBOOK PAGE 42**

Student Reader

Intermediate ESL Lesson Plans

A Conversational Approach

**Student
Workbook**

LESSON 1

EXERCISE 1: See Page 1 of the Student Reader. Answer these questions in sentences.

1. Where is Alex's new job?
   _____

2. Does Martha like her job?
   _____

3. What does Alex think about his present job?
   _____

4. What do you think Martha will say about moving to a small village?
   _____

5. Would you want to live in a small village?
   _____

6. Do you think that a small village would have a high school with a lot of athletic activities?
   _____

7. Do you enjoy athletic activities?
   _____

8. How old are pre-teen kids?
   _____

EXERCISE 2:   **MATCH THE MEANING**

a village _____   a job _____

to relocate _____   to be active _____

the present time _____   an opportunity_____

to bore _____   whether _____

twice _____   a disadvantage_____

    a bad thing
    to do many things
    a chance to do something different
    to go to live in a different place
    if

    your work
    a very small town
    two times
    to be uninteresting
    now

Student Worksheets

LESSON 1 CONTINUED

EXERCISE 3:

The letters "un" or "dis" in front of a word make it negative.

EXAMPLE: happy – unhappy   advantage - disadvantage

Make these words negative.

Add "un"   Add "dis"

available _____   agree   _____

clean   _____   please _____

interesting _____   respect _____

ACTIVITY 4: BRAINSTORM IN SMALL GROUPS

If you were Alex, what would be the advantages and disadvantages of moving to a small town?

ADVANTAGES   DISADVANTAGES

_____   _____

_____   _____

_____   _____

Every group is to list their advantages and disadvantages on the board
In the large group prioritize the advantages and disadvantages starting with the best one.

EXERCISE 4:   Complete the following:

1. If Martha has to stay in a small village, she will _____

2. If Alex has to commute, he _____

3. If the children have to move to a small village _____

4. If Martha has to give up her job _____

5. If Alex decided to take the job offer, he could _____

6. If you were Alex, what would you do? _____

Student Worksheets

LESSON 1 CONTINUED

ACTIVITY 6:   **DIVIDE INTO SMALL GROUPS:**

Alex receives the job offer. He is very happy about it, but he has to talk to Martha. He doesn't think that she will want to move to another place. Make a conversation about this.

ALEX: I just received a job offer! It is a much better job, and it pays a lot more money.

MARTHA: _____, but where is it?

ALEX: The job is in Southtown.

MARTHA: _____

ALEX: But it's only fifty kilometers away.

MARTHA: _____

ALEX: If we moved there, we could _____

MARTHA: _____

ALEX: I know so _____

ACTIVITY 7:   **BINGO**

DIRECTIONS: First, the students are to match the meaning by writing the number of the words in List 1 beside the meaning in List 2. EXAMPLE: 1. a very small town

Next, they are to write the **words** in List 1 into the BINGO squares.
The words should be placed randomly so that all of the printed cards are different.
The meanings in List 2 can then be called to begin playing the game as outlined below.

The teacher or a student can call the words in the WORDS TO CALL list, allowing the students time to find the matching word(s) among the ones that they have printed into the squares. Some help is given as the game is played, as the goal is for the students to learn the vocabulary.

For the first game, the students are to mark the matching word box with a small x
The winner(s) of the game call BINGO when they have a straight and complete row of x marked boxes. The marked rows can be in a straight vertical line, a straight horizontal line, or a straight diagonal line. The diagonal line must go from one corner to the other.

The FREE box is counted as a marked word when it is a part of the completed row.
The game can be played a number of times until the students know the vocabulary well. For each successive game, use a different symbol to mark the boxes.

Student Worksheets

LESSON 1 CONTINUED

BINGO

LIST 1
1. a village
2. your job
3. to relocate
4. to be active
5. the present time
6. an offer
7. to bore
8. an advantage
9. whether
10. a disadvantage
11. twice
12. to return
13. to be able
14. wine
15. different
16. downtown
17. to shop
18. a couple
19. a decision
20. to afford
21. airport
22. to leave
23. in advance
24. a bathing suit

LIST 2

a very small town
you decide what to
do your work
a bad thing
now
to depart
to be uninteresting
two times

to look for things to buy
two people or things
to move your home to a another place
to have enough money
where the planes are
an opportunity for something before
you wear it swimming

if
to do many things
a good thing
to come back can
you drink it
not the same
in town

Student Worksheets

LESSON 2

EXERCISE 1: Change the following sentences into the future progressive tense using, will be + the present participle
Remember – the present participle ends in "ing".

EXAMPLE:
I went to a volleyball game yesterday.   I'll be going to a volleyball game tomorrow.

1. I saw my friend Elizabeth yesterday.
   _____

2. I eat my dinner at one o'clock.
   _____

3. He is going to the lake today.
   _____

4. I finished my work at five o'clock.
   _____

5. They took many dogs to the forest.
   _____

6. She was reading many books.
   _____

EXERCISE 2: Phrasal Verbs Review

Phrasal verbs are a verb plus a preposition that, when put together, have a special meaning. You used these phrasal verbs in Module 2. Use them to complete the following sentences. Remember to use the right tense.

sleep in   stay up   right away   pick up   turn in   talk about   check in   give up

1. The travelers _____ to a hotel.

2. Sarah and Peter are determined to find new friends, so they will never _____.

3. She _____ her friend in her new red car.

4. They went to bed very late so they _____ the next morning.

5. Sarah and Peter _____ what they would do in the evening.

6. The party was a lot of fun so they _____ late.

7. They would be late if they didn't leave _____.

8. The girl found a wallet so she _____ it _____ to the police.

Student Worksheets

LESSON 2 CONTINUED

EXERCISE 3: Complete the following sentences using **will** and the future progressive tense. **EXAMPLE:** Anne writes a letter to her friend every day. Right now, she is writing a letter. At this time tomorrow she **will be writing** a letter.

1. Tom reads books every evening.
   Tomorrow evening he _____

2. Jim plays soccer early every morning.
   Next Monday morning he _____

3. Susan goes to dancing classes on Wednesdays and Fridays.
   Next Friday she _____

4. Bernard runs every morning.
   On Thursday morning he _____

5. Your country's athletes won some medals.
   In the future you hope
   they _____

EXERCISE 4:
Look for the words in Lessons 1 and 2.

ACROSS
1 to leave
3 to do a lot / to move a lot
5 a bird
6 not anything
9 to move to another place

DOWN
1 something that isn't good
2 two
4 a small town
7 someone who shoots animals or birds
8 it makes a car go
10 a small place full of water

Student Worksheets

LESSON 3

EXERCISE 1: Answer in sentences.

1. Are you going to be having a long weekend soon?
   _____

2. What you are going to be doing tomorrow?
   _____

3. Are you going to be getting information about a swim team?
   _____

4. Are you going to be going to a theater soon?
   _____

EXERCISE 2: Complete the dialogue

NARRATOR: Sarah and Peter are talking about finding a rowing or kayaking group in

PETER: Vancouver. How are we going to get some _____?

SARAH: Let's phone the Y. They're going _____ _____ starting a new semester soon.

PETER: Should I tell them what we are interested _____?

SARAH: Sure, find out what they _____ _____ _____ _____ offering.

NARRATOR: Peter phones.

PETER: The girl who answered says they _____ _____ _____ _____ printing the brochure for the next semester soon.

SARAH: Are they _____ _____ _____ including rowing and kayaking?

PETER: Yes, they'll send us the brochure in a couple of weeks.

Words to help you: is   are   going to be…   information

Student Worksheets

LESSON 3 CONTINUED

EXERCISE 3: Complete the following sentences using **(am / is / are) going to be)** and the future progressive tense.

NOTE: Some of these sentences could be completed using the simple future. For practice, please use the future progressive.

EXAMPLE: Jane goes swimming every Thursday.
Next Thursday she **is going to be going** swimming.

1. Mary gets home late on Fridays.

    Next Friday she _____

2. Jacob and Patrick catch fish in the river on Sundays.

    Next Sunday they _____

3. You go out on Saturdays.

    Where _____ next Saturday?

    (Answer) I _____

4. Margaret always waits five minutes for her friend, Jack.

    Tomorrow she _____ five minutes for Jack.

5. Richard always meets his girlfriend in the park on Sundays.

    Next Sunday Richard _____ his girlfriend in the park.

6. Susanna dances at the club on Saturdays.

    Susanna _____ at the club next Saturday.

7. Sarah has planned to go rowing with a group from the Y next semester.
Next semester Sarah _____ with a group from the Y.

Student Worksheets

LESSON 3 CONTINUED

EXERCISE 4:

ACROSS
1. stories and plays
3. the person responsible for
4. everything think
6. answer
9. a kind of boat
11. part of a school year
12. a place where people work
14. to get something for a good price

DOWN
1. poem
2. to make a boat move
5. the money you pay for things
7. someone who grows what we
8. eat people dance there
10. terrible
13. a kind of school

Student Worksheets

LESSON 4   REVIEW

EXERCISE 1:   **MATCH THE MEANING**

might   as   well   to pick up _____

_____ to pay for   next to   _____

_____ to leave   to decide   _____

for _____ to be   that suits me _____

to depart for _____   can choose to do something to give
to get someone or   money for something   I like that
something beside   why don't we?

EXERCISE 2:   Answer in sentences:

1. Are you going to be buying a baseball bat and ball tomorrow?
   _____

2. Will you be playing baseball this year?
   _____

3. Are you going to be riding a motorcycle tomorrow?_____

4. Will you be rowing with a group of friends next semester _____

5. Would you buy a motorcycle if you had enough money?_____

6. Are you going to be listening to the radio tonight _____

7. Will you be singing on the radio next week?_____

8. Would you go kayaking if your friends were going?_____

9. Would you phone the Y if you wanted to find a new group of friends?
   _____

Student Worksheets

LESSON 4 CONTINUED

ACTIVITY 5: Each student is to have a role card from the Guide, Pages 16 to 19.
Give out the role cards as shown in the Teacher's Guide.

For a class smaller than 19 students, the bottom sentences in the lists below will not be used.
One half of the students are to answer the questions in the GROUP 1 LIST.
The other half, are to answer the questions in the GROUP 2 LIST.
The students are to move about the classroom asking and answering each other.
When a student answers, then the student asking the question is to put the correct **role name** beside the item on their Group List.
Students should use the question and answer forms given below.
FIND SOMEONE WHO:

ASK: What are you going to be doing?   **ASK:** What will you be doing?

Role Name: Group 1 List   **Role Name: Group 2 List**

_____ is going to be playing tennis.

_____ is going to be golfing.

_____ will be swimming.

_____ is going to be running.

_____ is going to be going to the movies.

_____ is going to be reading.

_____ will be walking in the mountains.

_____ will be going to church.

_____ will be going to a restaurant.

_____ is going to be gardening. _____ will be boating.

_____ is going to be going fishing.

_____ is going to be watching television.

_____ will be listening to the radio.

_____ will be going dancing.

_____ is going to be playing the guitar.

_____ is going to be going to a party.

_____ will be going shopping.

_____ is going to be going to the theater.

_____ will be playing tennis. _____ will be golfing.

_____ is going to be swimming. _____ will be running.

_____ will be going to the movies.

_____ will be reading.

_____ is going to be walking in the mountains.

_____ is going to be going to church.

_____ is going to be going to a restaurant.

_____ will be gardening. _____ is going to be boating.

_____ will be going fishing.

_____ will be watching television. _____ is going to be listening to the radio.

_____ is going to be dancing.

_____ will be playing the guitar.

_____ will be going to a party.

_____ is going to be going shopping.

_____ will be going to the theater.

Student Worksheets

LESSON 5

EXERCISE 1: Answer these questions in sentences.

1. In what year was Lady Gaga born? _____
2. In her school years, did she fit in with the other girls? _____
3. Did she go to university? _____
4. Did Lady Gaga have a difficult time getting started? _____
5. Did her first contract bring her fame? _____
6. Did she work as a song writer? _____
7. Did her early, difficult working years lead to success?

_____

EXERCISE 2: Complete the sentences using these words:

strange   learned   fit in   experimenting   living

When Stefani Germanotta, later known as Lady Gaga, went to school, she didn't _____

_____. She dropped out of university to try to make a _____ with her music. She

wrote songs, and started her own band. In these early years, she _____ about the world

by wearing _____ clothing, _____ with drugs, and singing in bars.

ACTIVITY 3 - TEACHER'S GUIDE PAGE 25   FAMOUS PEOPLE

YOU ARE ALL VERY FAMOUS   FIND YOUR COLLEAGUES

Each student is given a role card. The students are to ask each other:
"Who are you?" and **"What do you do?"**

When they find someone who has the same Claim to Fame, they are to sit together and write a paragraph that tells:

- how long they have known each other
- where they met
- when they worked or competed together.

Student Worksheets

12

LESSON 5 CONTINUED

ACTIVITY 4:   **BINGO**

See the instructions for playing Bingo in Lesson 1 of this book. Before playing the game, the students are to write the number of the words in LIST 1 beside the words with the same meanings in List 2.

LIST 1   **MATCH THE MEANING**

overweight gain	born	fit in (to)	perform (to)
politics	it suits me	study (to)	social issues
shape	contract	forward	eccentric
(to) can	experiment	album	solve (to)
college	(to) manners	lonely	foreign
	fame	same as	information

LIST 2   **WORDS TO CALL:**

people know about you   how you act
facts about something   wanting a friend
to be liked by your friends   like
a collection of songs   to find a way to do something
to get more   government
to learn about   to try different things
something strange   how society is run
too heavy   to do something in front of an audience
to come into the world   a legal agreement
to give something form   a place of learning
from another country   I like that
to be able to   the way ahead

		BINGO		

Student Worksheets

LESSON 6

EXERCISE 1: Write questions about the pictures on Student Reader page 11 using "many" or "much" and the word in brackets. Use **"How"**, **"Is there"** or **"Are there"**.

EXAMPLE: (cars) How many cars are on the page?
(ladies) Are there many ladies?

1. (elephants) _____?
2. (strong men) _____?
3. (energy, strong man) _____?
4. (energy, weak man) _____?
5. (cats) _____?

EXERCISE 2: Use **"many"** or **"much"** in the following sentences.

1. There are _____ hats in the store
2. Was there _____ rain last month?
3. Did you eat _____ this morning?
4. There were _____ girls in town.
5. He ate _____ sandwiches.

6. Did you hear _____ singing?
7. He has _____ cousins.
8. Are there _____ people here?
9. Do you have _____ energy?

EXERCISE 3: Answer these questions using **much**, **many**, **a lot** or **a lot of**

1. Did you do much homework last night? _____
2. Did you see many birds yesterday? _____
3. Do you have much information about your country? _____
4. Does your family give you much advice? _____
5. Do you listen to much music? _____
6. Did you buy many apples last week? _____
7. Do you have much information about the buses in your town? _____

Student Worksheets

LESSON 6 CONTINUED

ACTIVITY 4: Work with a partner to write these questions and answer them using: "**much**" "**many**" or "**a lot of**" plus the noun in the box.

EXAMPLE:

slang
Is there **much** slang in your language?
yes, there is **a lot of** slang in our language. or
No, there isn't **much** slang in our language. No, there isn't **a lot of** slang in our language.

1. birds

Are there _____? (yes)

Answer _____.

2. coffee

Is there _____? (Yes)

Answer: _____.

3. cats

Are there _____?

(no)

Answer: _____.

4. music

Is there _____?

(Yes) Answer: _____.

5. bicycles

Are there _____? (yes)

Answer: _____.

Student Worksheets

LESSON 6 CONTINUED

EXERCISE 4: You can you do this crossword puzzle, can't you? _____

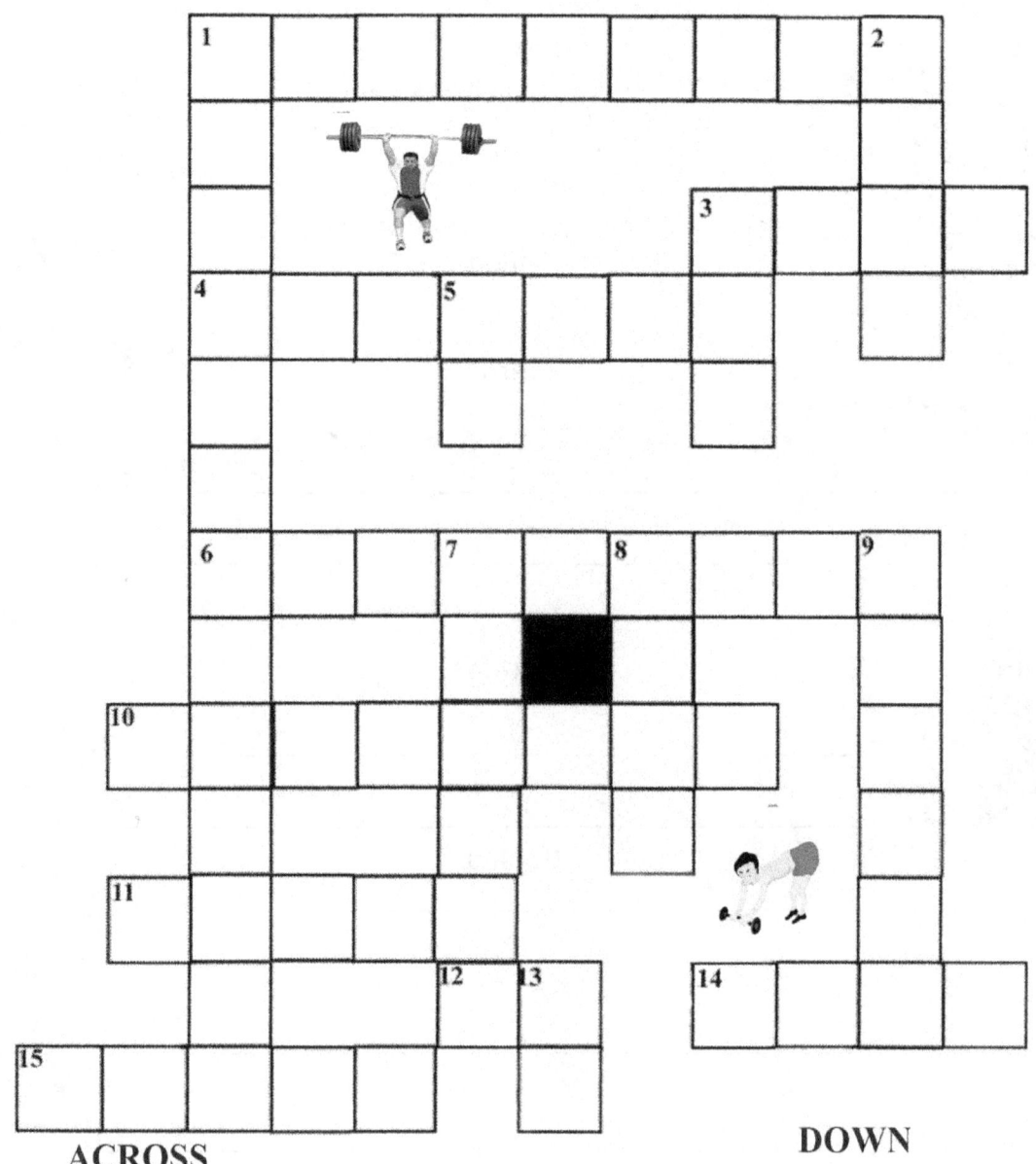

ACROSS

1. a famous person
3. the past tense of read
4. to tell people about something
6. about the spirit
10. the city or town where you were born
11. it's in lakes and rivers
12. not yes
14. the places around you
15. to think what could happen

DOWN

1. caring for other people
2. 365 days
3. a color
5. I
7. come back
8. a small city
9. small
13. a preposition

Student Worksheets

LESSON 7

SUBJECT AND OBJECT PRONOUNS

The pronouns below are the **subject** of the statement. (Subject pronouns)

I saw a new electric car.
Did **you** see it?
He / she / it / saw the new electric car. **One** often sees them.

We saw a new electric car.
You saw a new electric car.
They saw a new electric car.

The following pronouns are the **object** of the statement. (Object pronouns)
They can be used with or without a preposition.
Example: He worked for **them**. He helped **them**. **EXAMPLES:**

The prime minister doesn't know **me**. Does he know **you**?
My sister Maria worked for **him**.
He paid **her** well.
We searched until we found **it**.
I want a new car, but I don't have enough money to buy **one**.

The government works for **us**.
It makes laws are for all of **you**.
When we went there, we saw **them**.

EXERCISE 1: Complete the statements using an object pronoun.
EXAMPLE: Did you see **Jack**?
Yes, I saw **him**.

1. Did Sarah talk with Peter?
   Yes, she talked with _____.

2. Did your friends see you? (plural)
   Yes, they saw _____.

3. Did they find Mary?
   Yes, they found _____.

4. Did I give you the book?
   Yes, you gave _____ to _____.

5. This is Tony.
   Do you know _____?

6. This is Sarah and Peter.
   Do you know _____?

EXERCISE 2:

Answer in sentences using object pronouns instead of the **bold faced** words in your answer:

1. Do you like **hamburgers**?

   _____

2. Do you often eat **ice cream**?

   _____

3. Did you see **your friends** yesterday?

   _____

Student Worksheets

LESSON 7 CONTINUED

EXERCISE 3:   **Answer the questions in sentences.**

1. Was there ever a car run by a steam engine?
   _____

2. In 1900 were there many companies making cars?
   _____

3. When was the first electric car made?
   _____

4. Could the first electric cars travel very fast?
   _____

5. Why did the wealthy people like them?
   _____

6. Did you have to shift gears in electric cars?
   _____

7. Were electric cars popular with the ladies?
   _____

Student Worksheets

LESSON 8   REVIEW

EXERCISE 1:

Because gas powered cars cause so much pollution, the whole world is suffering from climate change. At the same time the price of gas and diesel fuel keeps going up. Many big companies are starting to use electric vehicles to deliver things. Many governments are changing all of their cars and trucks to electric vehicles.
Shipping goods across North America is a huge business. Already some companies are experimenting with huge trucks with electric motors. There is even talk of special roads for electric trucks. These trucks might travel in small groups with only one driver on these roads.

Divide into small groups and answer the questions, then each group read their answers to the class.

1. Gas and diesel vehicles cause a lot of air pollution. Name some other sources of air pollution.

2. In the early 1900's, having an electric car showed that you had money: it was a status symbol. In today's world, is the vehicle you drive still considered a status symbol?

3. If everyone switched to electric vehicles, what do you think the changes in society might be?

4. What kind of car would you like to own: a gas powered vehicle, or an electric car?

EXERCISE 2:

1. Do you have much time to watch TV?

   _____

2. Are there many parks in this city?

   _____

3. Do you eat much fruit?

   _____

4. Are there many students in this class?

   _____

5. Do you have much information about this city?

   _____

Student Worksheets

LESSON 8 CONTINUED

ACTIVITY 4: **WORK WITH A PARTNER:**
One person is to make the question using the given word. The other is to answer. Use "**much**" or "**many**" "**a lot**" or "**a lot of**" in your questions and answers. Marco and Simone looked at the following apartments:

APARTMENT 1: The building has ten floors. It is on a city street. It is a very busy street. Student 1: Are there **many** buses? Student 2: Yes, there are **many** buses.

EXAMPLE: buses

1. **trucks** Student1: _____?

   Student2: _____.

2. **noise** Student1: _____?

   Student 2: _____.

APARTMENT 2: The building is old and has three floors.
There are higher buildings nearby so the rooms don't get a lot of sunlight.
There is a high school with a playing field across the street.

3. **higher buildings**
Student 1: _____?

Student 2: _____.

4. **sunlight**
Student 1: _____?

Student 2: _____.

APARTMENT 3: This condo faces the ocean. There is a park across the street. It is near the mountains so it often rains. Ducks feed on the grass in the park. It is expensive.

5. **rain:** Student 1: _____?

   Student 2: _____.

6. **ducks:** Student 1: _____?

   Student 2: _____.

7. **money:** Student 1: _____?

   Student 2: _____.

Student Worksheets

LESSON 8 CONTINUED

EXERCISE 3: Perhaps you'll be famous one day. It's possible, so never give up!

ACROSS

1 to give up
5 a car or truck
8 not the same as others
11 not as expensive
12 up to date

DOWN

2 a funny play or movie
3 very strong
4 a place that makes things
6 people ride them
7 when people get married
9 from another country
10 a large group of people

Student Worksheets

LESSON 8 CONTINUED

EXERCISE 1: MATCH THE MEANING

a creature   _____

your   _____

community   _____

speed   _____

TV station   _____

strange   _____

space   _____

flashing   _____

officer   _____

a pilot   _____

wake up (to)   _____

rocket ship   _____

alien   _____

to broadcast   _____

planet
animal or alien
to send something by radio or television
a policeman
unusual
the place where you live
to stop sleeping
a light going on and off

where the television reporters work
someone from space
how fast you go
he or she drives something
where the moon and stars are
it flies through space
we live on one

EXERCISE 2: Answer in sentences:

1. Did you ever see a flying saucer?

   _____

2. Do you believe that aliens could visit our planet?

   _____

3. Did you hear reports of people seeing flying saucers?

   _____

Student Worksheets

LESSON 9

EXERCISE 3: Read your role-card several times so you know what happened to you.

Next, write the first sentence on your role-card below.
Remember, you have become that person, so change the pronoun!
Change what happened to you if you can. Write your story in your own words on the lines below. While the students study their roles the police are to record their questions below. The reporters are to sit together and plan their questions for a good story.

_____
_____
_____
_____
_____
_____
_____
_____
_____
_____
_____
_____
_____
_____

EXERCISE 4: You are telling your friend who didn't see the aliens about what happened to you. Complete your conversation.

You: Do you know _____?

Your friend: I heard about it on the television. Did you see anything?

You: _____
_____.

Your friend: Wow! What happened next?

You: _____.

Your friend: Cool! How did you feel after they flew away?

You: _____.

Your friend: I wonder if they'll come back? They might want to get more stuff.

You: _____.

Student Worksheets

LESSON 10

EXERCISE 1: MATCH THE MEANING

fans   _____

stands   _____

get out there _____

suddenly   _____

the stands   _____

buzzed   _____

working out   _____

an injured arm _____

pay it back   _____

stuff

someone's things	people who like the event	seats for seeing the
practicing with the other	the people in the stands	game go out with the
players to return something	talked it's difficult to use it	other players all at once

EXERCISE 2: Use these words to complete the paragraphs.

pitcher	manager	stuff	buzzed
second	tramp	made good	Yankees
chance	were out		
inning			

The Giants were working out with their _____, McGraw, when a man who

looked like a _____ walked onto the ball field. It was Jack Scott. He used to

be a great _____ before he injured his arm. He asked McGraw for a

_____ at playing with the team. Could he work out with the other players?

McGraw gave him $50.00 and told him to come back the next day and to bring his

_____.

Three months later the Giants were playing the _____. Suddenly McGraw

said, "Get out there, Scott. You're pitching today." The excited fans _____.

Could Scott pitch again? In the ninth _____ the Giants were leading 3 to 0.

Jack Scott was pitching. The first three players _____. Scott

_____ on his second chance by winning for the Giants!

Student Worksheets

LESSON 10 CONTINUED

EXERCISE 3: Answer these questions in sentences.

1. What month was it?
   _____

2. What game were they playing?
   _____

3. What did Jack Scott look like?
   _____

4. Why did Jack Scott stop pitching?
   _____

5. What kind of person was McGraw?
   _____

6. Why were the fans excited?
   _____

7. Did you ever have a second chance?
   _____

8. Did Scott make good on his second chance?
   _____

EXERCISE 4: Find the following kinds of sentences in the story.

1. Write a sentence that asks a question.
   _____

2. Write a sentence in the present tense.
   _____

3. Write a sentence in the past tense.

EXERCISE 5: Look in the story. Find words or groups of words with the opposite meaning.

after a long time _____

a rich man _____ a

didn't succeed _____

good arm _____

stay here _____

no hope _____

happy _____

Student Worksheets

LESSON 11

EXERCISE 1: **MATCH THE MEANING**

spirituals _____   to lead _____

pianist _____   pregnant _____

blues _____   weak _____

asleep _____   desolate _____

a storm _____   to combine _____

precious _____   an experience _____

    a time of difficulties or rain and   a sad kind of music
    wind   to show someone the way   to put things together
    expecting a child   something that happens to you
    religious songs   someone who plays the piano
    not strong   troubled / not knowing what to do
    something important to you   you are that way at night

EXERCISE 2:   Answer in sentences.

1. What does Ethan do?
   _____

2. What is important to him?
   _____

3. What gives him strength and hope?
   _____

4. How does he help the church?
   _____

5. Why can't the church pay him more money?
   _____

6. Why does he need more money?
   _____

7. What has he always studied?
   _____

8. Are most churches very poor?
   _____

Student Worksheets

LESSON 11 CONTINUED

ACTIVITY 6: **Divide into groups of three or four.**

Brainstorm what you think Ethan could do?
Remember that all ideas are to be accepted.
Funny ideas are often good ideas and make others think of new things.

1. He could become a rock singer.
2. He could find a church that could pay him a lot of money.
3. _____
4. _____
5. _____
6. _____

Return to the large group.
List the ideas of all the small groups on the blackboard and delete any doubles.
Read all the ideas aloud.

Return to the small group.
Discuss the ideas listed on the board and decide which one your group would choose.
You may want to use part of one idea and part of another.
Try to agree, but if someone thinks differently, they can report it to the large group.

Return to the large group.
Each small group plus anyone who had a different idea, is to report their decision to the class.

EXERCISE 3: **Write this paragraph in the past tense.**

Ethan is a gospel singer. The church is very important to him because it gives him strength and hope. He wants to help support the church with his singing but many churches are poor. They aren't able to pay him enough money for his wife and two children to live on. He has only studied singing.

_____
_____
_____
_____
_____
_____
_____

Student Worksheets

LESSON 12 REVIEW

ACTIVITY 3: Divide into groups of four or five.
Music is important to all of us.
If we are feeling sad, it can make us feel much better.
If we are going to be dancing, we couldn't do it without music. There are many different kinds of music for us to choose from.

Discuss the scenarios below and decide what kinds of music you would choose.

Think about how the people will want to feel.

Write your group's decision beside each scenario.

You are giving a party for your friends.
_____

You have a store that sells clothes for young people. They are usually between 14 and 24.
_____

Your uncle is sick so you want to make him feel better._____

You are planning the music that is played before a concert. (You decide what kind of concert) _____

You are planning the music for a library where people are reading.
_____

Student Worksheets

LESSON 12 CONTINUED

EXERCISE 1: Complete the sentences using object pronouns for the **bold faced** words.

1. Thousands of people listen to **gospel music**.

   Thousands _____

2. Sometimes it's very difficult to solve **problems**.

   Sometimes _____

3. One of the most beautiful gospel songs is by **Thomas Dorsey**.

   One of the most_____

4. Jack Scott pitched for the **fans**.

   Jack Scott _____

EXERCISE 2:   Using **and**, **but**, **or**, **so** to join the clauses.

EXAMPLES: She visited with her friends **and** they all went for a walk.
The train was slow **but** they enjoyed it.
They would enjoy traveling by plane **or** driving through the country by car. They didn't have enough money to travel far **so** they decided to stay at home.
     Join these sentences using **and**, **but**, **or**, **so**.
The examples will help you to remember how they are used.
Sometimes there is more than one correct way of joining the clauses.

1. I like listening to music. I have many CD's.

   _____

2. Blacks are very musical. They write their own songs.

   _____

3. People can sing in church. They can sing at home, too.

   _____

4. Thomas Dorsey was very sad. He started playing the piano.

   _____

5. The words and music that Dorsey wrote are very beautiful. Everyone enjoys them.

   _____

6. Mahalia Jackson sang gospel music on the radio. She often sang it in churches, too.

   _____

Student Worksheets

LESSON 12 CONTINUED

ACTIVITY 3: You'll find the words in Lessons 9 to 12.

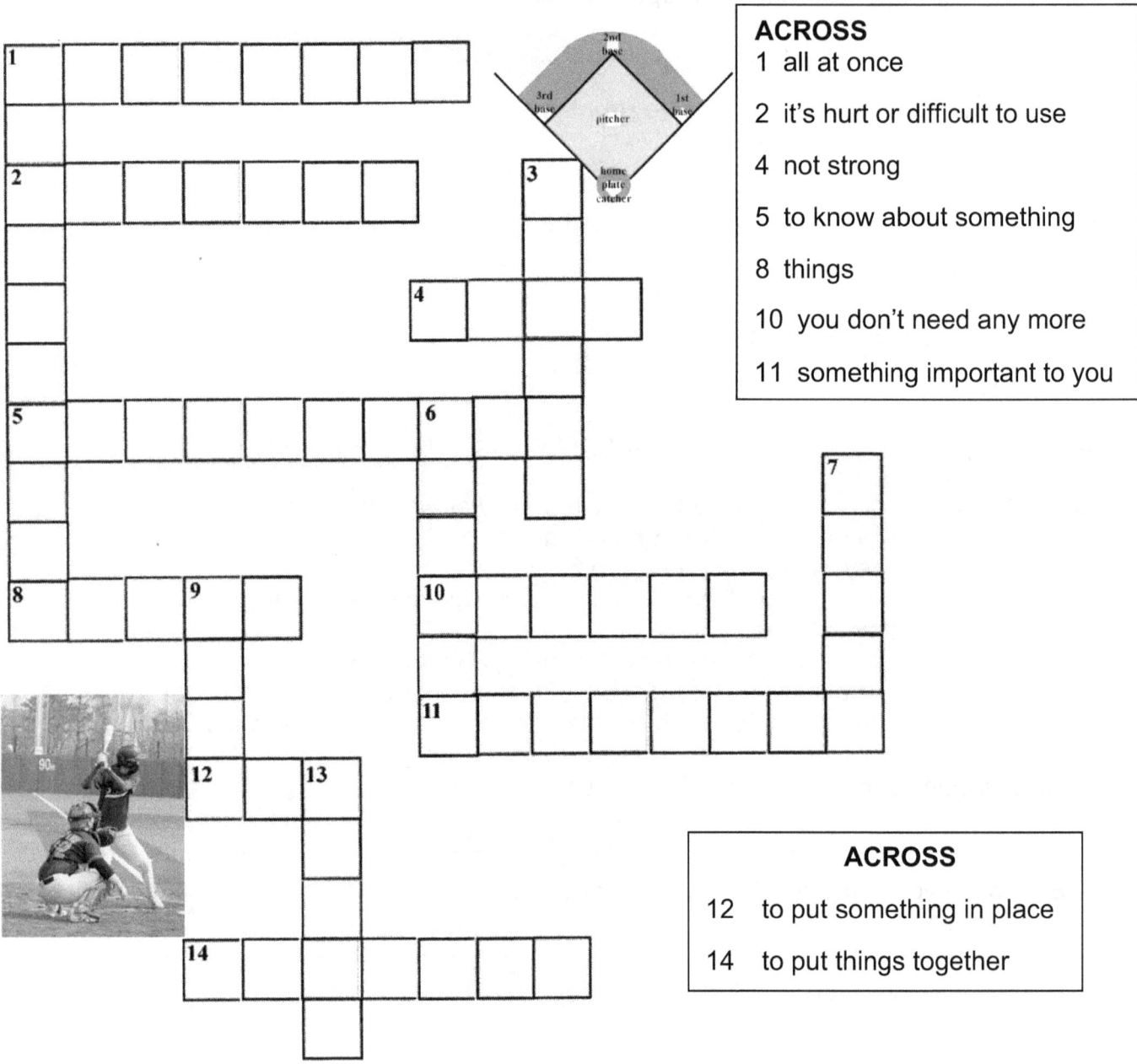

ACROSS
1 all at once
2 it's hurt or difficult to use
4 not strong
5 to know about something
8 things
10 you don't need any more
11 something important to you

ACROSS
12 to put something in place
14 to put things together

DOWN
1 religious songs
3 where the fans sit
6 you are that way at night
7 a kind of music
9 the people who sit in the stands
13 someone who is sad and poor

Student Worksheets

LESSON 13

EXERCISE 1:   **MATCH THE MEANING**

to influence a _____

century _____

to set an _____

example social _____

behavior _____

to pretend _____

to touch _____

poverty _____

to be acceptable _____

no money / poor
to teach something by doing it
to put your hand on something

actors do it well
to get people to think as you do
to do what your culture says is correct

100 years
what people do

EXERCISE 2:   **Answer in sentences.**

1. What family was the social leader of the British Empire?
   _____

2. What did Queen Victoria change when she became queen?
   _____

3. What was expected of the men?
   _____

4. What kind of clothes were the women to wear?
   _____

5. Did all the people really follow Queen Victoria's moral code?
   _____

6. Who suffered the most from her moral code?
   _____

Student Worksheets

LESSON 13 CONTINUED

EXERCISE 3:   Use the following phrases in sentences.
1. just pretended

   _____

2. the rest of

   _____

EXERCISE 4:   **PLURALS**

When a word ends in a consonant and "y", change the "y" to "i" and add "es".

EXAMPLE: century - centur**ies**

Make these words plural.

baby _____   opportunity _____

society _____   party _____

WORDS THAT SHOW OPPOSITION – THEY EXPRESS OPPOSITE IDEAS   whereas   but   on the other hand

EXAMPLES: Queen Victoria set a moral code, **but** many people didn't follow it. She thought she was right **whereas** they thought she was wrong. The rich had no problems. **On the other hand**, the poor suffered.

EXERCISE 5:   **Divide into groups of two or three.**

The society we live in today is very different from Queen Victoria's society. Compare the differences between Victoria's society and your society today. Complete the sentences using **whereas**, **but** or **on the other hand** for joining words.

1. Queen Victoria influenced the moral code of her times ...

   _____

2. The Royal family was the social leader ...

   _____

3. Men were expected to be at home with their families each evening...

   _____

4. Women were to wear clothes that covered their bodies...

   _____

5. Illegitimate children couldn't get good jobs when they became adults...

   _____

Student Worksheets

LESSON 13 CONTINUED

EXERCISE 6:
Must, have to, had to and have got to mean that something is very necessary.

EXAMPLES:
I **must** get up early tomorrow morning
I **have to** visit my old grandmother.
I **had to** visit my old grandmother.
I **have got to** visit my old grandmother.

Write sentences using these phrases beside the best form below.

have lunch	go to work
meet my friend at 9:00 PM	pay the restaurant bill
go to English class	go to the club
become a rock star	live in Queen Victoria's time
catch a bus	make a lot of money
listen more carefully	stop eating so much
get more exercise	save my money

must   I _____

have to   I _____

had to   I _____

have got to   I _____

will   I _____

going to   I am _____

would like to   I _____

we must they   We _____

have to   They _____

would like to   Most people _____

Student Worksheets

33

LESSON 14

EXERCISE 1: Answer the questions in sentences.

1. Whose son was Edward?
   _____

2. Before he was crowned, how did Edward spend his time?
   _____

3. What did the rich people do while Edward was king?
   _____

4. Who had all the power within British society?
   _____

5. Who tried to stop the men?
   _____

EXERCISE 2: MATCH THE MEANING

well known   _____

plenty   _____

power   _____

suffragettes   _____

the depression   _____
(1930's) in spite of   _____

rich   _____

bored   _____

to crown   _____

to attend   _____

USE THESE WORDS IN THE BLANKS

someone everyone knows   you can make people do what you want
women who wanted to vote   a lot
even though   people with a lot of money
a time when business was bad, people were not having enough to think about or do
hungry   to make a person king or queen   to go to

Student Worksheets

LESSON 14 CONTINUED

EXERCISE 3:   **ANSWER IN SENTENCES**

1. How old was Edward VII when he was crowned king?

   _____

2. Describe the times when Edward was king.

   _____

3. What did the people think of Edward VII?

   _____

4. Why is Edward's time known as the "Age of Men"?

   _____

5. What made the times between 1910 and 1945 difficult?

   _____

6. Would you want to live during the "Age of Men"?

   _____

EXERCISE 4:   **Combine the following sentences to make just one sentence:**

1. Edward became king at age 60. Only ruled the British Empire for eight years.

   _____

2. The Suffragettes fought for the vote. They wanted some of the power.

   _____

3. Edward couldn't become king until his mother died. He had a good time in Europe.

   _____

4. The suffragettes wanted to be able to vote. They wanted some of the power.

   _____

Student Worksheets

LESSON 14 CONTINUED

EXERCISE 5: The culture of Queen Victoria's times.

ACROSS

2 not down
6 needed
7 not late
8 one more than nine
10 very, very sad
12 one time
14 she wears a crown
15 inside

DOWN

1 children
3 it's not as it looks
4 what society says is right
5 a time when business was bad
8 a color
11 one less than two
13 to be able

Student Worksheets

LESSON 15

EXERCISE 1: **Answer the questions in sentences.**

1. What kind of a man was Edward?
   _____

2. Was he interested in government?
   _____

3. Why couldn't Wallis become queen?
   _____

4. How did Edward solve his problem?
   _____

EXERCISE 2   **MATCH THE MEANING**

to fall in love in spite of   _____

his heart's desire   _____

to forgive   _____

a violin   _____

| even though what he wanted the most | it's a musical instrument | to pardon |
| | in a short time you have a strong love for someone | |

EXERCISE 3:   **Some verbs are followed by an infinitive.**

EXAMPLES: **to decide** – Edward decided **to give** up his throne.
to pretend – Many people pretended **to follow** Queen Victoria's moral code. **to want** – Edward wanted **to marry** Wallis Simpson.

Write three sentences using **to decide, to pretend** and **to want** followed by an infinitive. Write sentences about things that are important to you so you will always remember them.

1. _____
2. _____
3. _____

Student Worksheets

LESSON 15 CONTINUED

ACTIVITY 4:   **Complete their dialogue.**

NARRATOR: A number of weeks later, Edward told the British people that he would marry Wallis Simpson. The people said they would never accept a divorced American as their queen. Edward and Wallis are alone. They plan their future.

EDWARD: Nothing will come between us.

WALLIS: The people will never_____.

EDWARD: You are right but _____.

WALLIS: How can you?

EDWARD: If I give up my_____.

WALLIS: Would you be happy?

EDWARD: Oh yes, my love. We will go_____.

WALLIS: But you are king of_____.

EDWARD: You are the most important to me. We will have parties and_____.

ACTIVITY 5:

The students will have sentences from page 57 of the Teacher's Guide that tell about the pictures on Pages 38, 39 and 40. They are to move about the room asking:

What does your sentence say?
The student asked, will read his/her sentence.

Then the student who asked the question is to look at the pictures until he /she finds the one that matches the sentence. He / She is to write the sentence under the picture.

_____   _____

_____   _____

Student Worksheets

LESSON 15 CONTINUED

_____
_____

_____
_____

_____
_____

_____
_____

_____
_____

_____
_____

_____
_____

_____
_____

Student Worksheets

LESSON 15 CONTINUED

_____   _____
_____   _____

_____   _____
_____   _____

_____
_____

Student Worksheets

LESSON 16

EXERCISE 1:   Make sentences of the following words:

1. moral, the, Queen Victoria, of, Empire, the, influenced, code, British

   _____

2. gave, kingdom, for, Edward, Wallis, a, up

   _____

3. twentieth, The, of, beginning, was, the, "Age of men", the, century

   _____

4. wanted, The, to, able, be, to, suffragettes, vote

   _____

EXERCISE 2:   Fill in the blanks using object pronouns for the bold faced words.

1. **Poor people** suffer from hunger if no one helps _____.

2. Edward VIII loved **Wallis Simpson**. He married _____.

3. Bill bought a **new car** last week. Did you see _____?

4. She has some **new books**. Did you see _____?

5. We saw the people there, but they didn't talk to **us**. Did they talk to _____?

Student Worksheets

EXERCISE 4:

LESSON 16 CONTINUED

ACROSS

2. the social order
3. to forget the past
5. to be poor
6. not strong
9. the way something should be done
11. also
12. Victoria sat on it

DOWN

1. a greeting
2. women who wanted the vote
4. to cast a ballot
5. to have lots
7. past tense of "to eat"
8. not enough money
10. It's in the sky at night

Student Worksheets

42

Intermediate ESL Lesson Plans

A Conversational Approach

STUDENT READER

LESSON 1

ORAL QUESTIONS
REVIEW OF MODULE 2

To the teacher: We suggest that you take time to do this review of Module 2 with the students. You can return to the lesson indicated in Module 2 if the students are having difficulty with a particular part. The review lessons in Module 1 are not included in this review. Assign the written exercises in Lesson 1 as homework if you are short of time.

Lesson 2
In what month is your national holiday?

What day of the month is Christmas?

*Our national holiday is **in** _____.*
*It's **in** _____.*
*Christmas is **on** December 25th.*
*It's **on** December 25th.*

Lesson 3
You're not a nurse, are you?
You eat dinner at noon, don't you?

You wear shoes to work, don't you?
You didn't get time off from work today, did you?

No, I'm not a nurse.
Yes, I do.
Yes, I eat dinner at noon.
Yes, I do.
No, I didn't.

Lesson 5
Do you live the same distance from school as ___?

Do you live as far from school as _____?

Yes, I live the same distance from school as _.
No, I don't live the same distance from…
Yes, I live as far from school as _____.
No, I don't live as far from school as ____.

Lesson 6
Do you like tennis better than basketball?
What drink do you like the best?

Yes, I like tennis better than basketball.
I like _____ the best.

Lesson 7
Are bicycles lighter than buses? Who came to class the earliest? Who came to class the latest?

Yes, bicycles are lighter than buses.
_____ came to class the earliest.
_____ came to class the latest.

Lesson 9
Lakes are wonderful, aren't they? She's beautiful, isn't she?

Yes, they are.
Yes, she's beautiful.

Lesson 10
Are you wearing a black jacket?

Does _____ have long hair?

Yes, I'm wearing a black jacket.
No, I'm not wearing a black jacket.
Yes, _____ has long hair.
No, _____ doesn't have long hair.

Teacher Guide

LESSON 1 CONTINUED

Lesson 11
Do you play basketball well?

Do you eat quickly?

Yes, I play basketball well.
No, I don't play basketball well.
Yes, I eat quickly.
No, I don't eat quickly.

Lesson 13
Do you sometimes take the bus?

Do you always wear shoes?

Yes, I sometimes take the bus.
No, I never take the bus.
Yes, I always wear shoes.
No, I don't always wear shoes.

Lesson 14
Do you ever have fruit for breakfast?

Do you ever buy coffee?

Yes, I sometimes have fruit for breakfast.
No, I don't ever have fruit for breakfast.
Yes, I buy coffee.
No, I don't ever / never buy coffee.

Lesson 15
Is it always dark at night?
Is the bus always crowded?

Is it ever cold in January?

Yes, it's always dark at night.
Yes, the bus is always crowded.
No, the bus isn't always crowded.
Yes, it is often cold in January.
No, it isn't ever cold in January.

Lesson 17
Would you like some chocolate? (plural)

Would they like some chocolate?

Yes, we'd like some chocolate.
No, we wouldn't like any chocolate.
Yes, they'd like some chocolate.
No, they wouldn't like any chocolate.

Lesson 18
Did you <u>talk about</u> a movie last night?

Do you <u>wait for</u> your friend every day?

Did you ever <u>compete in</u> a game?

Yes, I <u>talked about</u> a movie last night.
No, I didn't <u>talk about</u> a movie last night.
Yes, I <u>wait for</u> my friend every day.
No I don't <u>wait for</u> my friend every day.
Yes, I <u>competed in</u> a game.

Lesson 19
Have you got a pen in your pocket?

Have you got an interesting hobby?

Yes, I've got a pen in my pocket.
No, I haven't got a pen in my pocket.
Yes, I've got an interesting hobby.
No, I haven't got an interesting hobby.

Lesson 21
Do you enjoy English even though you're tired?
Do you enjoy athletic activities?

Yes, I enjoy English even though I'm tired.
No, I don't enjoy English when I'm tired.
Yes, I enjoy athletic activities.
No, I don't enjoy athletic activities.

Teacher Guide

LESSON 1 CONTINUED

Lesson 22
You won't miss the next class, will you?
You'd like to have a holiday, wouldn't you?

Lesson 23
Do you ever wear gloves?
Do you have a soft chair?

Lesson 25
Did you ever compete against another team?
Do you often think about your friends?

Lesson 26
If you were at a soccer game, would you cheer?

If you had a lot of money, what would you do?

Lesson 27
Would you want to be a pilot?

Do many planes take-off every day?

Lesson 29
How many toes do you have?
What do you wear on your feet?
Where is your nose?

Lesson 30
What helps you to smell?
Do you have a lot of teeth?

Lesson 31
Did you attend Live 8 in London?
Do you know many of the Beatle songs?

Lesson 33
Are there any snowy mountains in your country?
What would you want to do on your holiday?

No, I won't.
Yes, I would.

Yes, I sometimes wear gloves.
No, I never wear gloves.
Yes, I have a soft chair.
No, I don't have a soft chair.

Yes, I competed against another team.
No, I didn't ever compete against another…
Yes, I often think about my friends.
I think about many friends.
No, I don't think about my friends.

Yes, I'd cheer if I were at a soccer game.
No, I wouldn't cheer if I were at a soccer…
I'd _____ if I had a lot of money.

Yes, I'd want to be a pilot.
No, I wouldn't want to be a pilot.
Yes, many planes take-off every day.

I have ten toes.
I wear shoes on my feet.
My nose is on my face.

My nose helps me to smell.
Yes, I have a lot of teeth.
Yes, I have many teeth.

Yes, I attended Live 8 in London.
No, I didn't attend Live 8 in London.
Yes, I know many of the Beatle songs.
No, I don't know many of the Beatle songs.

Yes, there are some snowy mountains in my... No, there aren't any snowy mountains in my... I'd want to

_____.

Teacher Guide

LESSON 1 CONTINUED

Lesson 34
Do you frequently travel a long way?
Do you often take a bus?
Do you have many monuments in your city?

Yes, I frequently travel a long way.
No, I seldom / never travel a long way.
Yes, I often take a bus.
No, I never take a bus.
Yes, we have many monuments in our city. No, we don't have many monuments in our city.

Lesson 35
Can you drive a truck?
Do you ever go to the movies?

Yes, I can drive a truck.
No, I can't drive a truck.
Yes, I sometimes go to the movies.
No, I never go to the movies.

Lesson 37
Do you put food in a refrigerator?
Do you usually make a shopping list?

Yes, I put food in a refrigerator.
Yes, I usually make a shopping list.
No, I don't (usually) make a shopping list.

Lesson 38
Are you going to have a holiday soon?
Do you practice a sport with an instructor?

Yes, I'm going to have a holiday soon.
No, I'm not going to have a holiday soon.
Yes, I practice with an instructor.
No, I don't practice with an instructor.

Lesson 39
Do you ever ride a bicycle?
Are you taller than your friend is?

Yes, I ride a bicycle.
No, I don't ever ride a bicycle.
Yes, I'm taller than my friend is
No, I'm not taller than my friend is.

ORAL QUESTIONS FOR LESSON 1

Did you get an offer for (of) a better job?

Yes, I got an offer for (of) a better job.
No, I didn't get an offer for (of) a better job.

Do you like your job / school?

Yes, I like my job / school.
No, I don't like my job / school.

Do you live in a village?

Yes, I live in a village.
No, I don't live in a village.

How far from town do you live?

I live _____ kilometres from town.
I live in town.

Do you live as far from town as _____?

Yes, I live as far from town as _____.
No, I don't live as far from town as _____.

Have you ever relocated with your family?

Yes, I have relocated with my family.
No, I haven't ever relocated with my family.
No, I've never relocated with my family.

Are you active with a group?

Yes, I'm active with a _____ group.
No, I'm not active with a group.

Teacher Guide

LESSON 1 CONTINUED

PAGE 1   ANSWERS TO THE WORKBOOK QUESTIONS   EXERCISE 1:

1. Where is Alex's new job?
   It is in a small village fifty kilometers away.
2. Does Martha like her job?
   Yes, she likes / enjoys her job.
3. What does Alex think about his present job?
   He thinks it is boring.
4. What do you think Martha will say about moving to a small village?
   She'll say she doesn't want to leave her job.
   She'll say she doesn't want to live in a small village.
5. Would you want to live in a small village?
   Yes, I'd want to live in a small village.
   No, I wouldn't want to live in a small village.
6. Do you think that a small village would have a high school with a lot of athletic activities?*No, I don't think that a small village would have a high school with a lot of athletic activities.*
7. Do you enjoy athletic activities?
   Yes, I enjoy athletic activities.
   No, I don't enjoy athletic activities.
8. How old are pre-teen kids?
   Pre-teen kids are ten, eleven or twelve years old.
9. What are you very active in?
   I'm very active in …
   I'm not very active in anything.
10. Would you want to work in an office?
    Yes, I'd want to work in an office.
    No, I wouldn't want to work in an office.

PAGE 1   ANSWERS TO THE WORKBOOK QUESTIONS   EXERCISE 2:

a village	***a very small town***	a job	***your work***
to relocate	***to go to live in a different***	to be active	***to do many***
the present time	***place now***	an opportunity	***things a chance to do something different***
	to be uninteresting	whether	
to bore	***two times***	a disadvantage	***if***
twice			***a bad thing***

PAGE 2   ANSWERS TO THE WORKBOOK QUESTIONS   EXERCISE 3:

available	***unavailable***	agree	***disagree***
clean	***unclean***	please	***displease***
interesting	***uninteresting***	respect	***disrespect***

Teacher Guide

LESSON 1 CONTINUED

PAGE 2:   SUGGESTED ANSWERS TO THE WORKBOOK QUESTIONS   ACTIVITY 4:

ADVANTAGES	DISADVANTAGES
a more interesting	moving the family
job more money	changing Martha's job leaving
new friends	Martha's church group children
a quiet life	will miss their friends

PAGE 2   ANSWERS TO THE WORKBOOK QUESTIONS   EXERCISE 4:

1. If Martha has to stay in a small village, she will **be unhappy. / be bored.**
2. If Alex has to commute, he **will drive a long way each day.**
3. If the children have to move to a small village, **they will find new friends. / go to a new school**.
4. If Martha has to give up her job **she will need to find another one.**
5. If Alex decided to take the job offer, he could **make more money.**
6. If you were Alex, what would you do?

PAGE 3:   SUGGESTED ANSWERS TO THE WORKBOOK QUESTIONS   ACTIVITY 6:

Alex receives the job offer. He is very happy about it, but he has to talk to Martha. He doesn't think that she will want to move to another place. Make a conversation about this.

ALEX: I just received a job offer! It is a much better job, and it pays a lot more money.
MARTHA: That's great, but where is it?
ALEX: The job is in Churchtown.
MARTHA: That's a long way from here.
ALEX: But it's only fifty kilometers away.
MARTHA: Your gas would be expensive.
ALEX: If we moved there, we could have a better house. / buy some nice things.
MARTHA: I don't know what we should do. / I like living here.
ALEX: I know, so I think I'll have to commute. / I'll have to think about it.

PAGE 4   ANSWERS TO THE WORKBOOK   BINGO   ACTIVITY 7:

1	**a very small town**	17	to look for things to buy	9	if
19	you decide what to	18	two people or things	4	to do many things
2	do your work	3	to move your home to	8	a good thing
10	a bad thing		another place	12	to come back
11	two times	24	you wear it swimming	16	in town
5	now	20	to have enough money	6	an opportunity for
13	can	21	where the planes are	15	something not the same
22	to depart	14	you drink it	23	before
7	to be uninteresting				

Teacher Guide

LESSON 2

ORAL QUESTIONS

Will you be going to work tomorrow?	Yes, I'll be going to work tomorrow.
	No, I won't be going to work tomorrow.
Where will you be going after class?	I'll be going home.
	I'll be going to _____.
Will you be needing a car tonight?	Yes, I'll be needing a car tonight.
	No, I won't be needing a car tonight.

Will you be taking the bus tomorrow?	Yes, I'll be taking the bus tomorrow.
	No, I won't be taking the bus tomorrow.
Are you hoping to be at work on time?	Yes, I'm hoping to be at work on time.
Will you be eating dinner at noon tomorrow?	Yes, I'll be eating dinner at noon.
	No, I'll be eating dinner at _____.

Do you ever look for bargains?	Yes, I look for bargains.
	No, I don't (usually) look for bargains.
Are there some ducks on a pond near here?	Yes, there are some ducks on a pond near here.
	No, there aren't any ducks on a pond near here.
	No, there isn't a pond near here.
Do hunters shoot birds?	Yes, hunters shoot birds.

Does the hot weather suit you?	Yes, the very hot weather suits me.
	No, the very hot weather doesn't suit me.
Did you just move here?	Yes, I just moved here.
	No, I didn't just move here.
Do you want to find new friends?	Yes, I want to find new friends.
	No, I have many friends.

Do you have enough time to study English?	Yes, I have enough time to study English.
	No, I don't have enough time to study English.
Do some farmers have ducks?	Yes, some farmers have ducks.
	No, most farmers don't have ducks.
Do you shoot ducks?	Yes, I shoot ducks.
	No, I don't shoot ducks.

Do you have something in your bag?	Yes, I have something in my bag.
	No, I don't have anything in my bag.
	No, there's nothing in my bag.
Do you ever have nothing to do?	I (usually) have something to do.
	Sometimes I have nothing to do.
Will you be eating in a restaurant tonight?	Yes, I'll be eating in a restaurant tonight.
	No, I won't be eating in a restaurant tonight.

Teacher Guide

LESSON 2 CONTINUED

Photocopy this page and cut it into question cards. Divide the class into Team 1 and Team 2. Give each student one or two question cards. A student on Team 1 is to ask the question on his or her card to a student on Team 2. Then a student on Team 2 will ask someone on Team 1. Points can be given for correct answers. All students should ask and answer at least one question.

Do you ever meet new friends?
Yes, I meet new friends.
No, I don't ever meet new friends.

Are you a farmer?
Yes, I'm a farmer.
No, I'm not a farmer.

Will you be answering a question?
Yes, I'll be answering a question.
No, I won't be answering a question.

Do you put your books in a bag?
Yes, I put my books in a bag.
No, I don't put my books in a bag.

Do you ever shoot ducks?
Yes, I shoot ducks.
No, I don't shoot ducks.

Is there a pond near here?
Yes, there's a pond near here.
No, there isn't a pond near here.

Do you ever have duck for dinner?
Yes, I have duck for dinner.
No, I don't have duck for dinner.

Is there a church near here?
Yes, there's a church near here.
No, there isn't a church near here.

Would it suit you to have a glass of juice?
Yes, it would suit me to have a glass of juice. No, it wouldn't suit me to have a glass of juice.

Do you have enough time to study your English?
Yes, I have enough time to study my English.
No, I don't have enough time to study my English

Do you enjoy a glass of juice in the evening?
Yes, I enjoy a glass of juice in the evening.
No, I don't enjoy a glass of juice in the evening.

Are you a hunter?
Yes, I'm a hunter.
No, I'm not a hunter.

How much time do we have for this lesson?
We have ninety minutes for this lesson.
We have an hour and a half for this lesson.

Did you get a good bargain in town last week?
Yes, I got a good bargain in town last week.
No, I didn't get a good bargain in town last week.

Do you commute from another town each day?
Yes, I commute from another town each day.
No, I don't commute from another town each…

Teacher Guide

LESSON 2 CONTINUED

PAGE 5   ANSWERS TO THE WORKBOOK QUESTIONS   EXERCISE 1:

1. I saw my friend Elizabeth yesterday.
   I'll be seeing my friend Elizabeth tomorrow.
2. I eat my dinner at one o'clock.
   I'll be eating my dinner at one o'clock
3. He is going to the lake today.
   He'll be going to the lake today.
4. I finished my work at five o'clock.
   I'll be finishing my work at five o'clock.
5. They took many dogs to the forest.
   They'll be taking many dogs to the forest.
6. She was reading many books.
   She'll be reading many books.
7. They were enjoying a glass of juice.
   They'll be enjoying a glass of juice.

PAGE 4   ANSWERS TO THE STUDENT READER QUESTIONS   ACTIVITY 5:

1. **Do you know what you will be doing tomorrow?**
   Yes, I know what I'll be doing tomorrow.
   No, I don't know what I'll be doing tomorrow.
2. **Will you be playing volleyball on the beach tomorrow?** *Yes, I'll be playing volleyball tomorrow.*
   No, I won't be playing volleyball tomorrow.
3. **Will you be taking the bus to work in the morning?** *Yes, I'll be taking the bus to work in the morning.*
   No, I won't be taking the bus to work in the morning.
4. **Will you be going to a concert tonight?**
   Yes, I'll be going to a concert tonight.
   No, I won't be going to a concert tonight.
5. **Will you be getting married next week?**
   Yes, I'll be getting married next week.
   No, I won't be getting married next week.
6. **Will you be going to the movies tonight?**
   Yes, I'll be going to the movies tonight.
   No, I won't be going to the movies tonight.
7. **Will your friend be visiting you this weekend?**
   Yes, my friend will be visiting me this weekend.
   No, my friend won't be visiting me this weekend.
8. **Will you be going to town tomorrow?**
   Yes, I'll be going to town tomorrow.
   No, I won't be going to town tomorrow.
9. **Will you be buying a dog next week?**
   Yes, I'll be buying a dog next week.
   No, I won't be buying a dog next week.
10. **Will you be eating dinner at home tonight?**
    Yes, I'll be eating dinner at home tonight.
    No, I won't be eating dinner at home tonight.

Teacher Guide

LESSON 2 CONTINUED

PAGE 5   **ANSWERS TO THE WORKBOOK QUESTIONS**   **EXERCISE 2:**

1. The travelers **checked in** to a hotel.
2. Sarah and Peter are determined to find new friends, so they will never **give up**.
3. She **picked up** her friend in her new red car.
4. They went to bed very late so they **slept in** the next morning.
5. Sarah and Peter **talked about** what they would do in the evening.
6. The party was a lot of fun so they **stayed up** late.
7. They would be late if they didn't leave **right away**.
8. The girl found a wallet so she **turned** it **in** to the police.

PAGE 6   **ANSWERS TO THE WORKBOOK QUESTIONS**   **EXERCISE 3:**

1. Tom reads books every evening.
   Tomorrow evening he **will be reading a book.**
2. Jim plays soccer early every morning.
   Next Monday morning he **will be playing soccer.**
3. Susan goes to dancing classes on Wednesdays and Fridays. Next Friday she **will be going to a dancing class.**
4. Bernard runs every morning.
   On Thursday morning he **will be running.**
5. Your country's athletes won many medals.
   In the future you hope that they **will be winning many medals.**

PAGE 6   **ANSWERS TO THE CROSSWORD PUZZLE EXERCISE 4:**

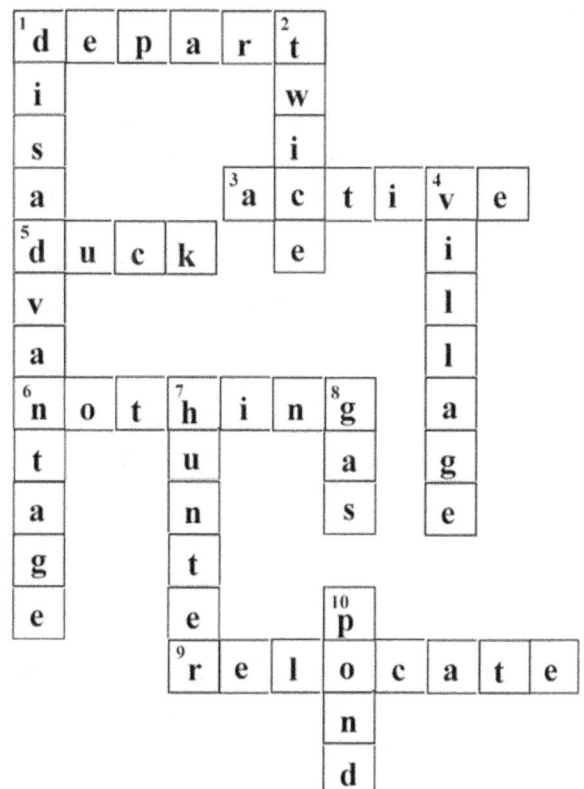

Teacher Guide

LESSON 3

To the teacher:

- Many of these questions could be correctly answered using "will" in the future progressive tense or by using the simple future. However, as it is difficult for the students to become comfortable with this form of the future progressive, they need a lot of oral practice. Ask these questions many times and then have them do the following activity.

ORAL QUESTIONS

Are you going to be going somewhere tonight?	Yes, I'm going to be going somewhere tonight. No, I'm not going to be going anywhere tonight. I'm going to be going to _____.
What are you going to be doing after class? Are you going to be getting home soon?	Yes, I'm going to be getting home soon. No, I'm not going to be getting home soon.
Are you going to be needing a car tomorrow?	Yes, I'm going to be needing a car tomorrow. No, I'm not going to be needing a car tomorrow.
Are you going to be studying tonight?	Yes, I'm going to be studying tonight. No, I'm not going to be studying tonight.
Are you going to be getting married tomorrow?	Yes, I'm going to be getting married tomorrow. No, I'm not going to be getting married…
Are you going to be seeing your friend tonight?	Yes, I'm going to be seeing my friend tonight. No, I'm not going to be seeing my friend tonight.
Are you going to be walking in the park today?	Yes, I'm going to be walking in the park today. No, I'm not going to be walking in the park…
Is your friend going to be studying English?	Yes, my friend is going to be studying English. No, my friend isn't going to be studying…
Are you going to be eating hotdogs every day?	Yes, I'm going to be eating hotdogs every day. No, I'm not going to be eating hot dogs every…
Are you going to be sleeping in tomorrow?	Yes, I'm going to be sleeping in tomorrow. No, I'm not going to be sleeping in tomorrow.
Are you going to be playing soccer today?	Yes, I'm going to be playing soccer today. No, I'm not going to be playing soccer today.
Are you going to be shopping tomorrow?	Yes, I'm going to be shopping tomorrow. No, I'm not going to be shopping tomorrow.

Teacher Guide

LESSON 3 CONTINUED

PAGE 7 **ANSWERS TO THE TEXTBOOK QUESTIONS** **EXERCISE 1:**

1. **Are you going to be having a long weekend soon?**
   Yes, I'm going to be having a long weekend soon.
   No, I'm not going to be having a long weekend soon.

2. **What are going to be doing tomorrow?**
   I'm going to be _____ tomorrow.
   I don't know what I'm going to be doing tomorrow.

3. **Are you going to be getting information about a swim team?** *Yes, I'm going to be getting information about a swim team. No, I'm not going to be getting information about a swim team.*

4. **Are you going to be going to a theater soon?**
   Yes, I'm going to be going to a theater soon.
   No, I'm not going to be going to a theater soon.

5. **Are you going to be phoning your friend tonight?**
   Yes, I'm going to be phoning my friend tonight.
   No, I'm not going to be phoning my friend tonight.

PAGE 7 **ANSWERS TO THE WORKBOOK QUESTIONS** **EXERCISE 2:**

Narrator: Sarah and Peter are talking about finding a rowing or kayaking group in Vancouver.
Peter: How are we going to get some ***information***?
Sarah: Let's phone the Y. They're going ***to be*** starting a new
Peter: semester soon. Should I tell them what we are interested ***in***?
Sarah: Sure, find out what they ***are going to be*** offering.
Narrator: Peter phones.
Peter: The girl who answered says they ***are going to be*** printing the brochure for the next semester soon.
Sarah: Are they ***going to be*** including rowing and kayaking?
Peter: Yes, they'll send us the brochure in a couple of weeks.

Teacher Guide

LESSON 3 CONTINUED

ACTIVITY 5:

The students are to sit in two rows (teams) facing each other. Give each student some questions to ask members of the other row (team). Points may be given for correct answers.

What time are you going to be going to class tomorrow?
I am going to be going to class at _____.

Are you going to be living here next year?
Yes, I'm going to be living here next year.
No, I'm not going to be living here next year.

Are you going to be eating at a restaurant next week?
Yes, I'm going to be eating at a restaurant next week.
No, I'm not going to be eating at a restaurant next week.

Are you going to be having a party on your birthday?
Yes, I'm going to be having a party on my birthday.
No, I'm not going to be having a party on my birthday.

Are you going to be going away in the summer?
Yes, I'm going to be going away in the summer.
No, I'm not going to be going away in the summer.

Are you going to be seeing a movie next week?
Yes, I'm going to be seeing a movie next week.
No, I'm not going to be seeing a movie next week.

Do you expect to be going to a party this year?
Yes, I expect to be going to a party this year.
No, I don't expect to be going to a party this year.

Are you going to be going to a nice restaurant this weekend?
Yes, I'm going to be going to a nice restaurant this weekend.
No, I'm not going to be going to nice restaurant this weekend.

Teacher Guide

LESSON 3 CONTINUED

When are you going to be going to bed tonight?
I'm going to be going to bed at _____ o'clock tonight.
I don't know when I'm going to be going to bed tonight.

Are you going to be taking an English course after Christmas?
Yes, I'm going to be taking an English course after Christmas.
No, I'm not going to be taking an English course after Christmas.
I don't know if I'm going to be taking an English course after Christmas.

Are you going to be talking to your friend tonight?
Yes, I'm going to be talking to my friend tonight.
No, I'm not going to be talking to my friend tonight.

Where are you going to be meeting your friend?
I'm going to be meeting my friend in town / at a football game.
I'm not going to be meeting my friend tonight.

Where are you going to be going for your holidays?
I'm going to be going to _____ for my holidays.
I'm not going to be going anywhere for my holidays.

Are you going to be shopping on the weekend?
Yes, I'm going to be shopping on the weekend.
No, I'm not going to be shopping on the weekend.

When are you going to be traveling to another country?
I'm going to be traveling to another country in _____ / next week. I'm not going to be traveling to another country .

How long are you going to be talking to your friends?
I'm going to be talking to my friends for / an hour / ten minutes.
I'm not going to be talking to my friends.
I don't know how long I'm going to be talking to my friends.

Are you going to be studying for a couple of weeks?
Yes, I'm going to be studying for a couple of weeks.
No, I'm not going to be studying for a couple of weeks.

Teacher Guide

LESSON 3 CONTINUED

PAGE 8   ANSWERS TO THE TEXTBOOK QUESTIONS   EXERCISE 3:

1. **Mary gets home late on Fridays.**
   Next Friday she *is going to be getting home late.*
2. **Jacob and Patrick catch fish in the river on Sundays.**
   Next Sunday they *are going to be catching fish.*
3. **You go out on Saturdays.**
   Where *are you going to be going* next Saturday?
   (Answer) I*'m going to be going to* _____.
4. **Margaret always waits five minutes for her friend Jack.**
   Tomorrow she *is going to be waiting for* five minutes for Jack.
5. **Richard always meets his girlfriend in the park on Sundays.**
   Next Sunday Richard *is going to be meeting* his girlfriend in the park.
6. **Susanna dances at the club on Saturdays.**
   Susanna *is going to be dancing* at the club next Saturday.
7. **Sarah has planned to go rowing with a group from the Y next semester.** Next semester Sarah *is going to be rowing* with a group from the Y.
8. **Peter has joined a kayaking group at the Y. It starts next semester.** Next semester Peter *is going to be kayaking* with a group from the Y.

PAGE 9   ANSWERS TO THE TEXTBOOK QUESTIONS   EXERCISE 4:

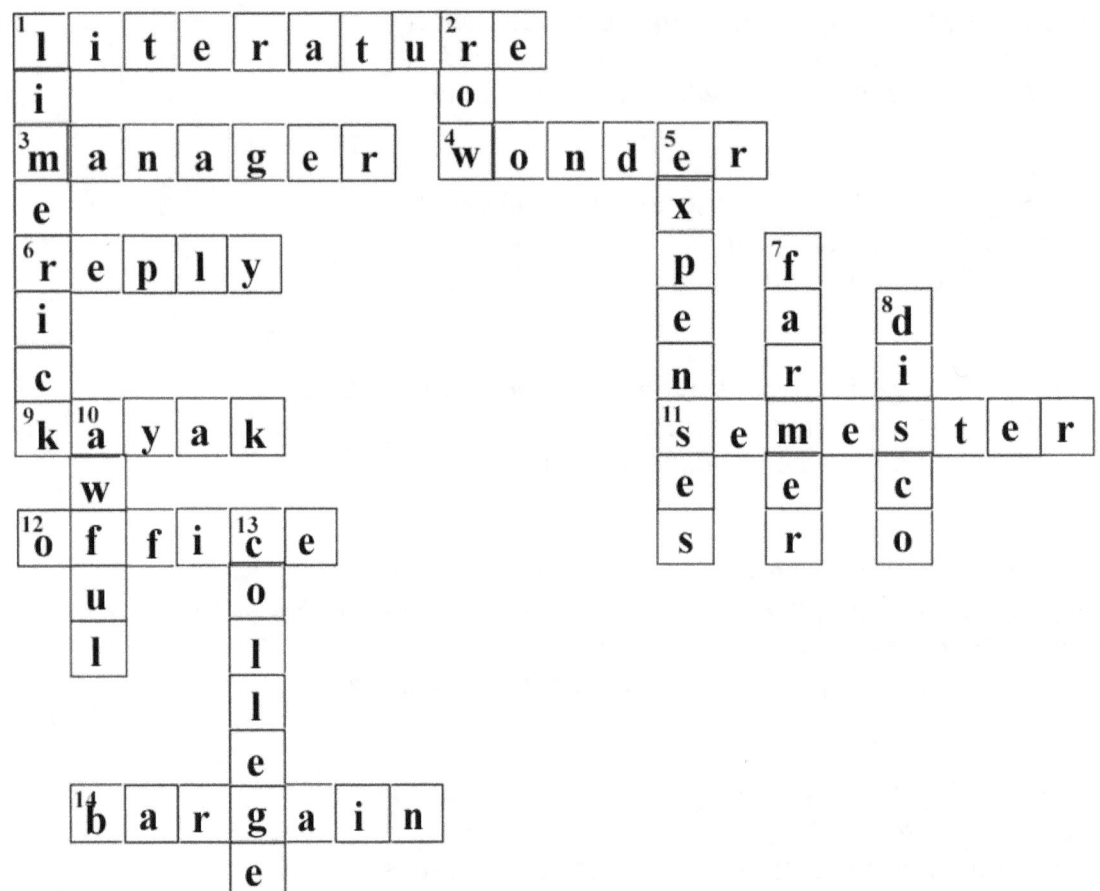

Teacher Guide

LESSON 4   REVIEW

ORAL QUESTIONS

Will you be seeing your mother tonight?	*Yes, I'll be seeing my mother tonight.* *No, I won't be seeing my mother tonight.*
When will you be going on holiday?	*I'll be going on holiday in _____.* *I won't be going on holiday.*
Will you be eating supper at home tonight?	*Yes, I'll be eating supper at home tonight.* *No, I won't be eating supper at home tonight.*
Will you be going to Canada next year?	*Yes, I'll be going to Canada next year.* *No, I won't be going to Canada next year.*
Are you going to be having some parties?	*Yes, I'm going to be having some parties.* *No, I'm not going to be having any parties.*
How will you be getting home tonight?	*I'll be getting home by bus / car / on foot.* *I'll not be going home tonight.*
Will it be getting warmer next month?	*Yes, it will be getting warmer next month.* *No, it won't be getting warmer next month.*
Will you be getting hungry tonight?	*Yes, I'll be getting hungry tonight.* *No, I won't be getting hungry tonight.*
Will you be going home after English class?	*Yes, I'll be going home after English class* *No, I won't be going home after...*
What are you going to be doing tonight?	*I'm going to be _____ tonight.*

ACTIVITY 5: To the teacher: The pictures for this activity are the same as the pictures for the Module 2 Lesson 38 activity but the student's task is very different. If a student receives the same picture as before, have him or her exchange with someone else.
The following pages have 19 role cards to go with this activity.

The role cards are to be distributed to the students as follows:

LEFT SIDE OF CLASSROOM	**RIGHT SIDE OF CLASSROOM**
Frances	Lawrence
Mary	Marion
Amanda	Stella
Muriel	Gordon
Stephen	Eddy
Claude	Monica Larry
Charlotte	Patsy
Edith	
Willy	

WILFRED
You really enjoy going to the theater. Sometimes you like to go to the movies and see a good film. You wish you had a friend to go to the movies and theater with. You also like to read.

In small classes, students may be given more than one role card.

Teacher Guide

LESSON 4 CONTINUED

FRANCIS Tennis is your game. You would love to find someone who could play a good game with you. Sometimes you like to play golf because being outside is important for you.

HARRY
You like being outside after working in an office all day. You play golf on the weekends and tennis after work. Although you'd like to have a regular partner for tennis, you usually meet someone when you go for a game.

MARY
You like to swim on the weekends. You belong to a competitive swimming group where you make many friends. You also enjoy running along quiet mountain trails.

LAWRENCE
Running helps you to plan your life. You like to run along the quiet mountain trails after each day's work. On the weekends you go to the church and then study your English at home.

AMANDA
You love going to the movies! You know about the lives of all the actors and actresses. You read books and magazines about the latest movies. You are also interested in clothes.

MARION
Your favorite hobby is reading magazines about the most popular actors and actresses. The magazine pictures help you to enjoy the movies that you attend every Saturday.

Teacher Guide

LESSON 4 CONTINUED

MURIEL
You work in an office all day. On the weekends you like to hike on the mountain trails. After work you often go swimming or play golf. You would like to meet someone who likes to do any of these things.

STELLA
After school you often walk to the church where it is peaceful and quiet. On the weekends you do a lot of reading and sometimes go skiing. You would like to go with a friend.

STEPHEN
You enjoy reading books about forests and gardening. On nice sunny spring days you like to work in your garden behind your house. You grow many vegetables and flowers.

GORDON
You work very hard all day. When you get home you are tired so you like to work in your garden or read a book. Sometimes you watch hockey on TV.

CLAUDE
You enjoy boating. You often like to take your boat to a quiet place where you can catch some fish. You'd like to find a friend who enjoys boating or fishing.

EDDIE
You really like fishing in the lake. You often wish you had a boat so you could go out where the big fish are. During the winter evenings you like to watch the hockey games.

Teacher Guide

LESSON 4 CONTINUED

CHARLOTTE
Outdoor sports are not for you! After work, you are tired. You just want to watch television or listen to the radio. You really enjoyed the Live 8 concerts and you were able to hear recordings of them all.

MONICA You are not the sporting kind.

You like to listen to the music on the radio. You enjoyed the Live 8 concerts on TV. You often go to the Temple to think about the meaning of life.

EDITH
You like going to parties. After work you often shop for new clothes to wear to the next party. You would like to find a friend who likes shopping and parties, too.

LARRY
You love to play hockey in the morning before you go to school. In the winter when the snow is deep and dry, you often go skiing on the nearby mountain.

WILLY
On the weekends you go skiing if there is enough snow on the nearby hills. You enjoy your work, but because you are sitting all day, you often go hiking along the nearby mountain trails after work

PATSY
You just love shopping! You read the magazines showing the latest clothes. Then you get excited about buying something new for the next party. You work hard because clothes are expensive. You wish you had a friend who liked shopping.

Teacher Guide

LESSON 4 CONTINUED

PAGE 7   IDEAS FOR THE STUDENT READER BRAINSTORMING ACTIVITY 1:

- they talked about their problem
- they shared their information about new situations
- they thought about others
- they used the telephone
- they gathered new information
- they thought about what would happen if they made specific changes
- they used community resources

PAGE 10   ANSWERS TO THE WORKBOOK QUESTIONS   EXERCISE 1:

might as well	*why don't we?*	pick up	*to get someone or something*
pay for	*to give money for*	next to	*beside*
leave for	*something to depart for*	decide to	*choose to do*
to be able to	*can*	that suits me	*something I like that*

PAGE 10   ANSWERS TO THE WORKBOOK QUESTIONS   EXERCISE 2:

1. **Are you going to be buying a baseball bat and ball tomorrow?**
   Yes, I'm going to be buying a baseball bat and ball tomorrow. No, I'm not going to be buying a baseball bat and ball tomorrow.

2. **Will you be playing baseball this year?**
   Yes, I'll be playing baseball this year.
   No, I won't be playing baseball this year.

3. **Are you going to be riding a motorcycle tomorrow?**
   Yes, I'm going to be riding a motorcycle tomorrow.
   No, I'm not going to be riding a motorcycle tomorrow.

4. **Will you be rowing with a group of friends next semester?**
   Yes, I'll be rowing with a group of friends next semester
   No, I won't be rowing with a group of friends next semester.

5. **Would you buy a motorcycle if you had enough money?**
   Yes, I'd buy a motorcycle if I had enough money.
   No, I wouldn't buy a motorcycle if I had enough money.

6. **Are you going to be listening to the radio tonight?**
   Yes, I'm going to be listening to the radio tonight.
   No, I'm not going to be listening to the radio tonight.

7. **Will you be singing on the radio next week?**
   Yes, I'll be singing on the radio next week.
   No, I won't be singing on the radio next week.

8. **Would you go kayaking if your friends were going?**
   Yes, I'd go if my friends were going.
   No, I wouldn't go if my friends were going.

9. **Would you phone the Y if you wanted to find a new group of friends?**
   Yes, I'd phone if I wanted to find a new group of friends.
   No, I wouldn't phone the Y if I wanted to find a new group of friends.

Teacher Guide

LESSON 4 CONTINUED

PAGES 15 TO 18   ANSWERS TO THE TEXTBOOK QUESTIONS   ACTIVITY 5:

Role Name   Group 1 List
What are you going to be doing?

Role Name   Group 2 List
What will you be doing?

Frances is going to be playing tennis.

Frances will be playing tennis.

Harry is going to be golfing.

Harry will be golfing.

Mary will be swimming.

Mary is going to be swimming.

Lawrence is going to be running.

Lawrence will be running.

Amanda is going to be going to the movies.

Amanda will be going to the movies.

Marion is going to be reading.

Marion will be reading.

Muriel will be hiking in the mountains.

Muriel is going to be hiking in the mountains.

Stella will be going to church.

Stella is going to be going to church.

Stephen will be growing vegetables.

Stephen is going to be growing vegetables.

Gordon is going to be gardening.

Gordon will be gardening.

Claude will be boating.

Claude is going to be boating.

Eddy is going to be going fishing.

Eddy will be going fishing.

Charlotte is going to be watching television.

Charlotte will be watching television.

Monica will be listening to the radio.

Monica is going to be listening to the radio.

Edith is going to be going to a party.

Edith will be going to a party.

Larry is going to be playing hockey.

Larry will be playing hockey.

Willy is going to be going skiing.

Willy will be going skiing.

Patsy will be going shopping.

Patsy is going to be going shopping.

Wilfred is going to be going to the theater.

Wilfred will be going to the theater.

Teacher Guide

LESSON 4 CONTINUED

ORAL QUESTIONS FOR TEST 1

1. Will you be playing volleyball today?
2. Are you going to be buying a motorcycle tomorrow?
3. If you moved to a small village, would you be happy?
4. Are you going to be going home at the end of this semester?
5. Are you looking forward to the weekend?

ANSWERS TO THE ORAL QUESTIONS FOR TEST 1

1. Yes, I'll be playing volleyball today.
   No, I won't be playing volleyball today.
2. Yes, I'm going to be buying a motorcycle tomorrow.
   No, I'm not going to be buying a motorcycle tomorrow.
3. If I moved to a small village, I would be happy.
   If I moved to a small village, I wouldn't be happy.
4. Yes, I'm going to be going home at the end of this semester.
   No, I'm not going to be going home at the end of this semester.
5. Yes, I'm looking forward to the weekend.
   No, I'm not looking forward to the weekend.

6. to pick up **to get**
7. that suits me **I like that**
8. .to want to **to like to**
9. to be able to **can**

10. next to **beside**
11. to leave for **to depart**
12. to relocate **to go to live in a different place.**

13. Yes, I'll be playing basketball tonight.
    No, I won't be playing basketball tonight.
14. Yes, I'm going to be buying a basketball tomorrow.
    No, I'm not going to be buying a basketball tomorrow.
15. If I went somewhere by plane, I would go to _____.
16. Yes, I would want to relocate to another city.
    No, I wouldn't want to relocate to another city.

Teacher Guide

LESSONS 1 TO 4   TEST 1 NAME _____

Answer the oral questions in sentences. (4 marks each)

1. _____
2. _____
3. _____
4. _____
5. _____

Match the meaning (2 marks each)

6. to pick up _____   10. next to _____

7. that suits me _____   11. to leave for _____

8. to want to _____   12. to relocate _____

9. to be able to _____

   to depart   to get   I like that
   to like to   can   beside
   to go to live in a different
   place

Answer in sentences (4 marks each)

13. Will you be playing basketball tonight?
    _____

14. Are you going to be buying a basketball tomorrow?
    _____

15. If you went somewhere by plane, where would you go?
    _____

16. Would you want to relocate to another city?
    _____

Teacher Guide

LESSON 5

ORAL QUESTIONS

Will you be listening to music tonight? — *Yes, I'll be listening to music tonight. / No, I won't be listening to music tonight.*

Are you going to be going to the cinema? — *Yes, I'm going to be going to the cinema. / No, I'm not going to be going to the cinema.*

Are you going to be going to a concert? — *Yes, I'm going to be going to a concert. / No, I'm not going to be going to a concert.*

Are you going to be singing tonight? — *Yes, I'm going to be singing tonight. / No, I'm not going to be singing tonight.*

Are you going to be a famous singer? — *Yes, I'm going to be a famous singer. / No, I'm not going to be a famous singer.*

Will you be watching a film tonight? — *Yes, I'll be watching a film tonight. / No I won't be watching a film tonight.*

Will you be seeing your friends tonight? — *Yes, I'll be seeing my friends tonight. / No, I won't be seeing my friends tonight.*

Will you be meeting a beautiful singer? — *Yes, I'll be meeting a beautiful singer. / No, I won't be meeting a beautiful singer.*

When do you listen to music? — *I listen to music in the evening/ all day/ at night.*

EXERCISE 1 WORKBOOK PAGE 12

1. In what year was Lady Gaga born?
   She was born in 1986.
2. In her school years, did she fit in with the other girls?
   No, she did not fit in with other girls.
3. Did she go to university?
   Yes, she went to university.
4. Did Lady Gaga have a difficult time getting started?
   Yes, she had a difficult time getting started.
5. Did her first contract bring her fame?
   No, it did not bring her fame.
6. Did she work as a song writer?
   Yes, she worked as a song writer.
7. Did her early, difficult working years lead to success?
   Yes, her early years led to success.

EXERCISE 2 WORKBOOK PAGE 12

When Stefani Germanotta, later known as Lady Gaga, went to school, she didn't **_fit in_**.

She dropped out of university to try to make a **_living_** with her music. She wrote songs, and started her own band. In these early years, she **_learned_** about the world by wearing **_strange_** clothing, **_experimenting_** with drugs, and singing in bars.

Teacher Guide

LESSON 5 CONTINUED

ACTIVITY 3:   FAMOUS PEOPLE

Note to the teacher: Be sure to give out the roles so that each person gets a partner.

EXAMPLE: Lynn Nash and Brooke Patterson have the same Claim to Fame. They are both car racers. The students with those Role Cards will have to find each other. If you have an odd number of students in the class, use:

Rocky Road, Sally Ray and Antoinette de Lovely because they are all authors.

or

Deborah Mills, Joseph Comero and Bert Skala because they are all politicians.

These would make one or two groups of three.

(m/f) = male or female

NAME: Lynn Nash
MARITAL STATUS: married
YEAR OF BIRTH: 1980
CLAIM TO FAME: car racing

NAME: Brooke Patterson (m/f)
MARITAL STATUS: single
YEAR OF BIRTH: 1984
CLAIM TO FAME: car racing

NAME: Ivan Zander
MARITAL STATUS: divorced
YEAR OF BIRTH: 1979
CLAIM TO FAME: actor/actress

NAME: Adrian (Adrianne) May
MARITAL STATUS: married
YEAR OF BIRTH: 1981
CLAIM TO FAME: actor/actress

NAME: Chris Patton (m/f)
MARITAL STATUS: married
YEAR OF BIRTH: 1985
CLAIM TO FAME: singing Celtic music

NAME: Penny Cuthbert
MARITAL STATUS: married
YEAR OF BIRTH: 1979
CLAIM TO FAME: singing Celtic music

NAME: Bruce Robertson
MARITAL STATUS: single
YEAR OF BIRTH: 1982
CLAIM TO FAME: dancing

NAME: Miranda Bates
MARITAL STATUS: single
YEAR OF BIRTH: 1981
CLAIM TO FAME: dancing

NAME: Alan Dunning
MARITAL STATUS: divorced
YEAR OF BIRTH: 1979
CLAIM TO FAME: football

NAME: Winston Donovan
MARITAL STATUS: single
YEAR OF BIRTH: 1982
CLAIM TO FAME: football

Teacher Guide

LESSON 5 CONTINUED

NAME: Daniela Black
MARITAL STATUS: single
YEAR OF BIRTH: 1979
CLAIM TO FAME: tennis

NAME: Elizabeth Fraser
MARITAL STATUS: married
YEAR OF BIRTH: 1984
CLAIM TO FAME: tennis

NAME: Linda Watts
MARITAL STATUS: single
YEAR OF BIRTH: 1986
CLAIM TO FAME: basketball

NAME: Kirk Vernon
MARITAL STATUS: single
YEAR OF BIRTH: 1982
CLAIM TO FAME: basketball

NAME: Rocky Road
MARITAL STATUS: single
YEAR OF BIRTH: 1987
CLAIM TO FAME: author

NAME: Sally Ray
MARITAL STATUS: married
YEAR OF BIRTH: 1982
CLAIM TO FAME: author

NAME: Antoinette De Lovely
MARITAL STATUS: divorced
YEAR OF BIRTH: 1979
CLAIM TO FAME: author

NAME: Joseph Comero
MARITAL STATUS: single
YEAR OF BIRTH: 1979
CLAIM TO FAME: politician

NAME: Deborah Mills
MARITAL STATUS: single
YEAR OF BIRTH: 1975
CLAIM TO FAME: politician

NAME: Bert Skala
MARITAL STATUS: married
DATE OF BIRTH: 1976
CLAIM TO FAME: politician

WORKBOOK PAGE 13   ANSWERS TO THE BINGO   ACTIVITY 4:

18	where you catch a train or bus	1	**Monday to Friday.**
14	your father's sister	9	perhaps
2	the month after February	13	you walk up or down them
4	they grow food there what	5	helps you when you aren't
8	you did in the water	15	well to decide on
11	going to different places	19	your uncle's child
17	you listen to it	21	you think with it
16	very old	20	joined together
6	seven days.	22	where you buy things
23	a movie	10	what you do at night
3	they are doctors for	24	thirty days
7	animals your mother's brother.	12	your evening meal

Teacher Guide

LESSON 6

ORAL QUESTIONS

MANY

How many students are here today?	There are _____ students here today. Yes, I have many holidays.
Do you have many holidays?	No, I don't have many holidays
Do you have many pens?	Yes, I have many pens.
	No, I don't have many pens.
Do you go to many concerts?	Yes, I go to many concerts.
Are there many restaurants in town?	No, I don't go to many concerts.
Are there many tables in this room?	Yes, there are many restaurants in town.
Do you have many husbands/wives?	Yes, there are many tables in this room.
Do you have many cousins?	No, I don't have many…
	Yes, I have many cousins.
	No, I don't have many cousins.

MUCH

A LOT OF   A LOT

Do you spend much money on bus tickets?

Yes, I spend a lot of money on bus tickets.
No, I don't spend much (a lot of) money on bus...
Yes, we had a lot of rain last year.

Did we have much rain last year?

No, we didn't have much (a lot of) rain last year.
Yes, I spend a lot of money on food.

Do you spend much money on food?

No, I don't spend much (a lot of) money on food.
Yes, I drank a lot of coffee yesterday.

Did you drink much coffee yesterday? Did

No, I didn't drink much (a lot of) coffee yesterday.

you do much gardening?

Yes, I did a lot of gardening.
No, I didn't do much (a lot of) gardening.

Yes, it costs a lot of money to go swimming.

Does it cost much money to go

No, it doesn't cost much (a lot of) money to go…
Yes, coffee costs a lot.

swimming? Does coffee cost much?

No, coffee doesn't cost much (a lot).

Yes, there were many people in town today.

Were there many people in town today?

No, there weren't many people in town today.
Yes, there are many people in this class.

Are there many people in this class?

No, there aren't many people in this class.
Yes, a dog has many (a lot of) teeth.

Does a dog have many teeth?
Did you get much mail yesterday?

Yes, I got a lot of mail yesterday.

Do you have a lot of money?

Yes, I have a lot of money.
Yes, I have lots of money.
No, I don't have much money.

Teacher Guide

LESSON 6 CONTINUED

PAGE 14   ANSWERS TO THE WORKBOOK QUESTIONS   EXERCISE 1:

1. How many elephants are on the page? / Are there many elephants on the page?
2. How many strong men are on the page? Is there a strong man are on the page?
3. How much energy does the strong man have?
4. How much energy does the weak man have? Does the weak man have much energy?
5. Are there many cats on this page? How many cats are on this page?

PAGE 14   ANSWERS TO THE WORKBOOKBOOK QUESTIONS   EXERCISE 2:

1. There are ***many*** hats in the store.
2. Was there *** much *** rain last month?
3. Did you eat *** much *** this morning?
4. There were *** many *** girls in town.
5. He ate *** many *** sandwiches.
6. Did you hear *** much *** singing?
7. He has *** many *** cousins.
8. Are there *** many *** people here?
9. Do you have *** much *** energy?

PAGE 14   ANSWERS TO THE TEXTBOOK QUESTIONS   EXERCISE 3:

1. Yes, I did a lot of homework last night.
   No, I didn't do much homework last night.
2. Yes, I saw many / a lot of birds yesterday.
   No, I didn't see many / a lot of birds yesterday.
3. Yes, I have a lot of information about our country.
   No, I don't have a lot of (much) information about our country.
4. Yes, my family gives me a lot of advice.
   No, my family doesn't give me a lot of (much) advice.
5. Yes, I listen to a lot of music.
   No, I don't listen to much / a lot of music.
6. Yes, I bought many / a lot of apples / last week.
   No, I didn't buy many / a lot of apples last week.
7. Yes, I have a lot of information about the buses in my town.
   No, I don't have much / a lot of information about the buses in my town.

PAGE 15   ANSWERS TO THE WORKBOOK QUESTIONS ACTIVITY 4:

Are there many birds?	No, there aren't many birds.
Are there a lot of birds?	No, there aren't a lot of birds.
Is there a lot of coffee in our country? Is there much coffee in our country?	Yes, there is a lot of coffee in our country. Yes, we have a lot of coffee.
Are there many cats?	No, there aren't many cats.
Are there a lot of cats?	No, there aren't a lot of cats.
Is there much music?	Yes, there is a lot of music.
Is there a lot of music?	Yes, there is a lot of music.
Are there many bicycles?	Yes, there are many bicycles. Yes, there are a
Are there a lot of bicycles?	lot of bicycles.

Teacher Guide

LESSON 6 CONTINUED

PAGE 16   ANSWERS TO THE WORKBOOK QUESTIONS   EXERCISE 4:

			¹c	e	l	e	b	r	i	t	²y	
			o								e	
			m				³r	e	a	d	
		⁴p	r	o	⁵m	o	t	e		r		
		a			e			d				
		s										
	⁶s	p	i	⁷r	i	⁸t	u	a	⁹l	
	i			e	■	o			i	
¹⁰h	o	m	e	t	o	w	n		t	
	n				u		n		t	
	¹¹w	a	t	e	r				l	
	t			¹²n	¹³o		¹⁴a	r	e	a
¹⁵g	u	e	s	s		f				

ACTIVITY 5: This is a whole class activity.
The students are to sit in two rows (teams) facing each other. Give each student some questions to ask members of the other row (team). Points may be given for correct answers.

Do you listen to a lot of Popular music? *Yes, I listen to a lot of Popular music.*
Yes, I listen to some Popular music.
No, I don't listen to a lot of Popular music.

Did Lady Gaga win many awards?
Yes, she won many awards.
Yes, she won a lot of awards.

Are there many different kinds of music? *Yes, there are many different kinds of music.*

Do many people listen to rock music? *Yes, many people listen to rock music.*
No, not many people listen to rock music.

Teacher Guide

LESSON 6 CONTINUED

Do we grow much coffee in this country?
Yes, we grow a lot of coffee in this country.
No, we don't grow a lot of coffee in this country.
No, we don't grow any coffee in this country.

Does your homework take much time?
Yes, my homework takes a lot of time.
No, my homework doesn't take much / a lot of time.

Did you buy many bananas at the store?
Yes, I bought many / a lot of bananas at the store.
No, I didn't buy many / a lot of bananas at the store.

Were there many people in town?
Yes, there were many / a lot of people in town.
No, there weren't many / a lot of people in town.

Did you drink a lot of coffee last night?
Yes, I drank a lot of coffee last night.
No, I didn't drink a lot of coffee last night.

Are there many people in this class?
Yes, there are many people in this class.
No, there aren't many people in this class.

Does it take you much time to get to class?
Yes, it takes me a lot of time to get to class.
No, it doesn't take me much time to get to class.

Do you have much information about Japan?
Yes, I have a lot of information about Japan.
No, I don't have much / a lot of information about Japan.

Are there many students in this school?
Yes, there are many / a lot of students in this school. No, there aren't many / a lot of students in this school.

LESSON 7

ORAL QUESTIONS

Are electric cars a new idea? — No, electric cars are not a new idea.
Could the early electric cars travel fast? — No, they could not travel fast.
Did you have to shift gears in the first electric cars? — No, you didn't have to shift gears.

Were electric cars popular at first? — Yes, they were very popular.
Did they become a status symbol? — Yes, they became a status symbol.
Were electric cars easy to drive? — Yes, they were very easy to drive.
Why did the ladies like electric cars? — They liked them because you didn't have to crank them.
You didn't have to shift gears. They were quieter.

What did Oliver Frichle's factory make?
Was he successful?
Were cars with gas engines smelly?
Did electric cars make a lot of noise?
Why weren't cars with steam engines popular? Henry Ford started using "mass production"
in his factory. What does this mean?

It made electric cars.
Yes, his factory made many cars.
Yes, they were very smelly.
No, they were quiet.
It took too long to make enough steam.

Each worker did just one thing as the car moved slowly past.

Did mass production bring down the cost of Ford's cars? — Yes, it brought down the cost.

Was Ford's factory more efficient than Frichle's factory. — Yes, it was much more efficient.

How much did Ford's Model T car cost in 1908? — It cost $650.00
Did the Frichle electric car cost more than the Ford car? — Yes, it cost much more.

Why did people prefer the Ford car? — It was so much cheaper than the electric car.

PAGE 17   ANSWERS TO THE WORKBOOK QUESTIONS.   EXERCISE 1:

EXAMPLE: Did you see Jack? Yes, I saw him.

1. Did Sarah talk with Peter?   Yes, she talked with **him**.
2. Did your friends see you? (plural) Yes, they saw **us**.
3. Did they find Mary?   Yes, they found **her**.
4. Did I give you the book? Yes, you gave **it** to **me**.
5. This is Tony.   Do you know **him**?
6. This is Sarah and Peter.   Do you know **them**?

Teacher Guide

LESSON 7 CONTINUED

PAGE 17   ANSWERS TO THE WORKBOOK QUESTIONS.   EXERCISE 2:

1. Do you like **hamburgers**?
    *Yes, I like **them**. No, I don't like **them**.*
2. Do you often eat **ice cream**?
    *Yes, I often eat **it**. No, I don't often eat **it**.*
3. Did you see **your friends** yesterday?
    *Yes, I saw **them** yesterday. No, I didn't see **them** yesterday.*

*Yes, I heard **them** barking last night.*
*No, I didn't hear **them** barking last night.*

PAGE 18   ANSWERS TO THE WORKBOOK QUESTIONS.   EXERCISE 3:

1. Was there ever a car run by a steam engine?
    Yes, there was a car made that was run by a steam engine.
2. In 1900 were there many companies making cars?
    Yes, there were many companies making cars.
3. When was the first electric car made?
    The first electric car was made in 1890.
4. Could the first electric cars travel very fast?
    No, they couldn't travel very fast.
5. Why did the wealthy people like them?
    They liked them because it showed that they had lots of money. (They became a status symbol.)
6. Did you have to shift gears in electric cars?
    No, you didn't have to shift gears.
7. Were electric cars popular with the ladies?
    Yes, they were popular with the ladies.
8. Are electric cars quieter than gas powered cars?
    Yes, they are much quieter than gas powered cars.
9. Why did people stop buying the early electric cars?
    People found gas powered cars much cheaper.
10. Do you think that electric cars will become more popular than gas powered cars?
    Yes, I think electric cars will become more popular than gas powered cars.

Teacher Guide

LESSON 8 — REVIEW

ORAL QUESTIONS

Will you be buying an electric car?	Yes, I'll be buying an electric car. No, I won't be buying an electric car.
Are you going to be driving an electric car?	Yes I'm going to be driving an electric car. No, I'm not going to be driving an electric car.
Are you going to be going to work tomorrow?	Yes, I'm going to be going to work tomorrow. No, I'm not going to be going to work tomorrow.
Are you going to be buying an electric car?	Yes, I'm going to be buying an electric car. No, I'm not going to be going out tonight.
Are you going to work in a factory?	Yes, I'm going to work in a factory. No, I'm not going to work in a factory.
Is your family going to be moving to Spain?	Yes, my family is going to be moving to Spain. No, my family isn't going to be moving to...
Are you frequently able to visit your friend?	Yes, I'm frequently able to visit my friend. No, I'm not frequently able to visit my friend.
Are you worried about where to live?	Yes, I'm worried about where to live. No, I'm not worried about where to live.
Do you buy much fruit each week?	Yes, I buy a lot of fruit each week. No, I don't buy much (a lot of) fruit each week.
Do we have much rain each year?	Yes, we have a lot of rain each year. No, we don't have much (a lot of) rain each…
Do you need much money for food?	Yes, I need a lot of money for food. No, I don't need much (a lot of) money for food.
Did you drink much coffee yesterday?	Yes, I drank a lot of coffee yesterday. No, I didn't drink much (a lot of) coffee ...
Did you do much gardening?	Yes, I did a lot of gardening. No, I didn't do much gardening.
Did you see a film last week?	Yes, I saw a film last week. No, I didn't see a film last week.
Do you have many clothes?	Yes, I have a lot of clothes. No, I don't have many clothes
Do you eat much bread?	Yes, I eat a lot of bread. No, I don't eat a lot of bread.
Do you have many sisters?	Yes, I have a lot of sisters. No, I don't have many sisters. No, I don't have any sisters.
Do you work a lot?	Yes, I work a lot. No, I don't work much.

Teacher Guide

LESSON 8 CONTINUED

PAGE 16   ANSWERS TO STUDENT READER QUESTIONS.   ACTIVITY 1:

1. Do you think President Biden was right when he said: *"The future of the auto industry is electric?"* **Yes, I think he was right.**
2. What does *"There is no turning back"* mean?
   It means we must keep going in the same direction.
3. Is the American government going to help the auto industry change to making electric cars?
   Yes, it is going to help the auto industry.
4. Why are bus companies switching to electric buses?
   It is cheaper to run electric buses.
5. Do you think the high price of gas will make people think about buying an electric vehicle?
   Yes, I think it may make people buy electric vehicles.

PAGE 19   ANSWERS TO THE WORKBOOK QUESTIONS.   EXERCISE 1:

1. Gas and diesel vehicles cause a lot of air pollution. Name some other sources of air pollution.
   Other sources: aeroplanes, ships, factories.
2. In the early 1900's, having an electric car showed that you had money: it was a status symbol. In today's world, is the vehicle you drive still considered a status symbol?
   Yes, cars and trucks are today's status symbols.
3. If everyone switched to electric vehicles, what do you think the changes in society might be?
   There would be less pollution, less sickness, and maybe stop the damage of climate change.
4. What kind of car would you like to own: a gas powered vehicle, or an electric car?
   I would like to own an electric vehicle.

PAGE 19   ANSWERS TO THE WORKBOOK QUESTIONS.   EXERCISE 2:

1. Do you have much time to watch TV?
   Yes, I have a lot of time to watch TV. No, I don't have much time to watch TV.
2. Are there many parks in this city?
   Yes, there are many parks in this city. No, there aren't many parks in this city.
3. Do you eat much fruit?
   Yes, I eat a lot of fruit. No, I don't eat much / a lot of / fruit.
4. Are there many students in this class?
   Yes, there are many students in this class. |
   No, there aren't many students in this class.
5. Do you have much information about this city?
   Yes, I have a lot of information about this city.
   No, I don't have much information about this city.

PAGE 20   ANSWERS TO THE WORK BOOK QUESTIONS   ACTIVITY 4:

1. Are there many / a lot of trucks?   *Yes, there are many / a lot of trucks.*
2. Is there much / a lot of noise?   *Yes, there is a lot of noise*
3. Are there many / a lot of higher buildings?   *Yes, there are many / a lot of higher buildings.*
4. Is there much / a lot of sunlight?   *No, there isn't a lot of sunlight. No, there isn't much sunlight.*
5. Is there much / a lot of rain?   *Yes, there is a lot of rain.*
6. Are there many / a lot of ducks?   *Yes, there are many / a lot of ducks.*
7. Do they need much / a lot of money?   *Yes, they need a lot of money.*

Teacher Guide

LESSON 8 CONTINUED

PAGE 21   ANSWERS TO THE WORKBOOK QUESTIONS.   EXERCISE 3:

ORAL QUESTIONS FOR TEST 2
1. Are you going to be playing volleyball tonight?
2. Does it take you much time to get to class?
3. Do you eat a lot of fruit?
4. Does the ocean have much water?
5. Do you worry about your English?

Answers to the oral questions.
1. Yes, I'm going to play volleyball tonight.   No, I'm not going to play volleyball tonight.
2. Yes, it takes me a lot of time to get to class.   No, it doesn't take me much time to get to class.
   No, it doesn't take me a lot of time to get to class.
3. Yes, I eat a lot of fruit.   No, I don't eat a lot of fruit.
   No, I don't eat much fruit.
4. Yes, the ocean has <u>a lot of</u> water.
5. Yes, I worry about my English.
   No, I don't worry about my English.

ANSWERS TO TEST 2
6. Yes, I will be eating my supper in a restaurant tomorrow. No, I won't be eating my supper in a restaurant tomorrow.
7. Yes, I have a lot of homework to do.
   No, I don't have much (a lot of) homework to do.

8. Adam is going to **_leave for_** Ecuador tomorrow.
9. Evelyn wanted to live with her children for **_the rest of_** her life.
10. When are you going to **_pick up_** your friend?
11. It is late at night so he will **_turn off_** the lights.
12. This jacket **_suits me_** so I'll buy it.
13. The man had to **_pay for_** his food.

Marie has an offer **_of / for_** a better job but it is far **_from_** her home. The job pays more **_than_** her present job but she doesn't want **_to_** move. Her boyfriend lives nearby and if she moved, she wouldn't **_be_** able **_to_** see him **_as_** often **_as_** she does now. However, if she decides **_to_** move she will get more money and the job will be **_much_** more interesting.

Teacher Guide

LESSONS 5 TO 8 **TEST 2 NAME** _____

Answer the oral questions in sentences. (4 marks each)

1. _____

2. _____

3. _____

4. _____

5. _____

Answer in sentences. (4 marks each)

6. Will you be eating your supper in a restaurant tomorrow?
   _____

7. Do you have much homework to do?
   _____

Complete the sentences using the following words. (2 marks each)

the rest of   turn off   leave for   pay for   suits me   pick up

8. Adam is going to _____ Ecuador tomorrow.

9. Evelyn wanted to live with her children for _____ her life.

10. When are you going to _____ your friend?

11. It is late at night so he will _____ the lights.

12. This jacket _____ so I'll buy it.

13. The man had to _____ his food.

Complete the paragraph using the following words: (1 mark each)

You may use the words more than once.

than   much   be   from   to   as   of   for

Marie has an offer _____ a better job but it is far _____ her home. The job pays more _____ her present job but she doesn't want _____ move. Her boyfriend lives nearby and if she moved, she wouldn't _____ able _____ see him _____ often _____ she does now. However, if she decides _____ move she will get more money and the job will be _____ more interesting.

Teacher Guide

LESSON 9

ALIENS   ACTIVITY 3:

INSTRUCTIONS: Give each student a role-card. Use them in the order listed below. We suggest that you assign two policemen. The police will talk together to decide what questions they will ask and record them in their workbooks. The reporters (there could be more for a large group) should do the same. The other students will need time to study their role-cards and write their story in their workbook in their own words. They should be encouraged to change the story on their role-card. Explain that copying it won't help them with their English.

ROLE-CARDS

You are a policeman / woman. You were driving through town when you were called on your radio to see about a flying saucer and some aliens that have landed nearby. Some of the people are reporting crazy things like green puppies and stolen dishes! You will have to ask people some questions. Try asking
"When…?" and "Why…?" Listen to what the people tell the reporters. Try to find out what really happened. Write more questions in your workbook as you listen to the others.

You are a television reporter. You are in the neighborhood to take pictures and find out what happened when the flying saucer landed. Listen to what the people tell the police then ask your own questions. You want to get the truth. Try asking "What…?" and "Where…?" As you listen, write some questions in your workbook so you are ready when it's your turn to ask.

You are a newspaper reporter. You are in the neighborhood where the flying saucer and the aliens landed. You want to have a good story to write. You don't care if it isn't true. Ask the students to tell you more. Try asking: "What…?" and How…?" Write questions in your workbook as you listen to the others so you'll be ready when it's your turn.

You were at home washing the dishes. Suddenly there was a loud noise. There was a red light. You ran outside and saw a space ship landing in your garden. Three strange green creatures got out. One of them saw you - he had a gun – there was a flash! The next thing you knew you were on your back in the garden. Was it a dream? When you went back into the kitchen you couldn't find your dishes!!

You were in your room playing a computer game. Suddenly two strange green men came into your bedroom. You heard a shot! When you woke up you remembered the green men. Now you can't play your computer game. It won't work!!

You were in your bedroom playing your favorite rock music. Your brother came running into your room talking about green men. You didn't hear everything he said so you told him he was playing too many computer games. Then you heard your mother and father. They were upset because your father didn't believe anything about the space ship and lunch wasn't ready.

When you came home for lunch your family was crazy! Your wife talked about a spaceship in the garden and some green men who shot her. One son said some green men shot him and now his computer game won't work. Your other son didn't hear anything because he was listening to rock music. You decided to buy your lunch but when you got into your car it wouldn't start.

Teacher Guide

LESSON 9 CONTINUED

You were in a field taking your dog for a walk. All at once your dog started to cry. You heard a noise and then the sky was filled with red light. Your dog was going crazy. Then she had her puppies and all of them were green!

You saw everything from your bedroom window. You heard a noise and a thing like a saucer flew past your window and landed in your neighbor's garden. Three green creatures that looked like people with big ears and without any hair got out. You saw one of them shoot your neighbor. Two of them went into the house and one walked around the garden. After a few minutes the other two came back to the ship carrying something but you couldn't see what. Then the ship flew away.

You were outside putting your clothes up to dry. You saw a spaceship coming closer and closer. Its flashing red light grew brighter. It was making your clothes dance up and down. As the ship got closer the clothes danced more and more, you couldn't move! You fell down. When you woke up your clothes were gone. Now you have no underwear!

You were out for a morning walk. Suddenly there was a flashing orange light. A great saucer shaped thing came over your head. An orange light was all around you and you couldn't move. Then your hat flew off your head and seemed to go into the ship. Don't these green men have any hats?

You were standing on the grass in your garden. You felt sleepy but just as you were going to sit down to sleep you saw a saucer shaped thing fly over your head. You thought you were dreaming but when you looked down you were standing in your underpants! Your pants were gone!!

You were watching the news on television. Suddenly you seemed to be watching a show about flying saucers. It looked like the saucer was in your neighborhood. There were strange men taking things. They took one lady's washing, someone else's hat and another person's shoes. Then they took one poor man's pants! Had some aliens taken control of the TV station?

PAGE 22   ANSWERS TO THE WORKBOOK QUESTIONS   EXERCISE 1:

a creature	an animal or alien
your	the place where you live
community	how fast you go
speed	where the television reporters work
TV station	unusual
strange	where the moon and stars are
space	a light going on and off
flashing	a policeman
officer	he or she drives something
a pilot	to stop sleeping
wake up (to)	it flies through space
rocket ship	someone from space
alien	to send something by radio or
to broadcast	television we live on one
planet	

Teacher Guide

LESSON 10

Notes to the teacher: We understand that many of the students won't be familiar with baseball. However, as they learn English, it is important that they learn a little about the culture of the English speaking countries. Baseball is a North American game. If the batter hits the ball he or she must run to as many bases as possible without being tagged by a player who has the ball. The player is safe while touching a base. He or she can continue trying to run home while the next batter is up at bat.

The <u>past perfect tense</u> hasn't been introduced but has been used with regular nouns in several stories. Encourage the students to understand the meaning through the context. The grammar will be taught later.

ORAL QUESTIONS

Do you play baseball in your country?
    Yes, we (I) play baseball in my country.
    No, we (I) don't play baseball in my country.

What does the baseball pitcher do?
    He or she throws the ball.
What does the catcher do?
    He or she catches the ball if the batter doesn't hit it.
Are people unhappy if no one wants them?
    Yes, they are very unhappy.

Do you have tramps in your country?
    Yes, we have tramps in our country.
    No, we don't have tramps in my country.

Does a cheap room cost a lot of money? Did you ever have a second chance?
    No, a cheap room doesn't cost a lot of money.
    Yes, I had a second chance.
    No, I never had a second chance.

Do you have a pocket?
    Yes, I have a pocket.
If you had $50.00 in your pocket would you give it away?
    Yes, I'd give it away.
    No, I wouldn't give it away.

Do you bring a lot of stuff to class?
    Yes, I bring a lot of stuff to class.
    No, I don't bring a lot of stuff to class.
Did you ever go to a baseball game?
    Yes, I went to a baseball game.
    No, I didn't ever go to a baseball game.
Did you ever win a game?
    Yes, I won a game.
    No, I never / haven't ever won a game.

Did you ever injure yourself?
    Yes, I've injured myself.
    No, I haven't ever injured myself.

PAGE 24   ANSWERS TO THE WORKBOOK QUESTIONS   EXERCISE 1:

fans	people who like the event
stands	seats for seeing the game
get out there	go out with the other players
suddenly	all at once
the stands	the people in the stands
buzzed	talked
working out	practicing with the other players
an injured arm	it is difficult to use it
pay it back	to return something
stuff	someone's things

Teacher Guide

LESSON 10 CONTINUED

PAGE 24   ANSWERS TO THE WORKBOOK QUESTIONS   EXERCISE 2:

The Giants were working out with their **_manager_**, McGraw, when a man who looked like a **_tramp_** walked onto the ball field. It was Jack Scott. He used to be a great **_pitcher_** before he injured his arm. He asked McGraw for a **_second chance_** at playing with the team. Could he work out with the other players? McGraw gave him $50.00 and told him to come back The next day and bring his **_stuff_**.

Three months later the Giants were playing the **_Yankees_**. Suddenly McGraw said, "Get out there, Scott. You're pitching today." The excited fans **_buzzed_**. Could Scott pitch again?

In the ninth **_inning_** the Giants were leading 3 to 0. Jack Scott was pitching. The first three players **_were out_**. Scott **_made good_** on his second chance by winning for the Giants!

PAGE 25   ANSWERS TO THE WORKBOOK QUESTIONS   EXERCISE 3:

1. **What month was it?**
   It was July.
2. **What game were they playing?**
   They were playing baseball.
3. **What did Jack Scott look like?**
   He looked like a tramp.
4. **Why did Jack Scott stop pitching?**
   He injured his arm. / He had an injured arm.
5. **What kind of person was McGraw?**
   He was kind hearted.
6. **Why were the fans excited?**
   They were excited because Jack Scott had come back.
7. Did **you ever have a second chance?**
   Yes, I had a second chance. No, I never had a second chance.
8. **Did Scott make good on his second chance?**
   Yes, he did.

PAGE 25   ANSWERS TO THE WORKBOOK QUESTIONS   EXERCISE 4:
   The students are to choose sentences from the story.

PAGE 25   ANSWERS TO THE WORKBOOK QUESTIONS   EXERCISE

			5: *suddenly*
a rich	*a tramp*	after a long	
man a	*a bad arm*	time didn't	*won*
good arm	*a second*	succeed stay	
no hope	*chance*	here	*get out there*
happy	*unhappy*		

Teacher Guide

LESSON 11

ORAL QUESTIONS

Do you enjoy gospel music?	Yes, I enjoy gospel music.
	No, I don't enjoy gospel music.
	I don't listen to gospel music.
Would you like to write a song?	Yes, I'd like to write a song.
	No, I wouldn't like to write a song.
Are there many churches in your country?	Yes, there are many churches in my country.
	No, here aren't many churches in my country.
Do some singers make a lot of money?	Yes, they make a lot of money.
	No, they don't make much money.
Can songs change the way people think?	Yes, they can change the way people think No, they can't change the way people think. Yes,
Do many people listen to music?	many people listen to music.
	No, not many people listen to music.
Do some singers compose music?	Yes, some singers compose music.
	No, most singers don't compose music.
What kind of music do you like the best?	I like _____ the best.
Do many people go to church / the temple?	Yes, many people go to church / the temple.
	No, most people don't go to church / the temple.
Do you listen to much music?	Yes, I listen to a lot of music.
	No, I don't listen to much music.
	No, I don't listen to a lot of music.
Do you enjoy many kinds of music?	Yes, I enjoy many kinds of music.
	No, I only enjoy a few kinds of music.
Are you a musician?	Yes, I'm a musician.
	No, I'm not a musician.
Do songs make people think?	Yes, they make some people think.
	No, songs don't make people think.
Do most people have problems?	Yes, most people have problems.
Can others help you to solve your problems?	Yes, others can help me to solve my problems.
	No, others can't help me to solve my problems.
	Yes, I think the rich people have problems.
Do you think the rich people have problems?	No, I don't think the rich people have problems.
	Yes, I've been out in a storm.
	No, I haven't ever been out in a storm.
Have you ever been out in a storm?	Yes, I combine working and studying.
	No, I don't combine working and studying. Yes,
Do you combine working and studying?	I'm usually asleep at night.
	No, I'm often awake at night.
Are you usually asleep at night?	

Teacher Guide

LESSON 11 CONTINUED

PAGE 26   ANSWERS TO THE WORKBOOK QUESTIONS   EXERCISE 1:

spirituals	*religious songs*
pianist	*someone who plays the piano*
blues	*a sad kind of music*
asleep	*you are that way at night*
a storm	*a time of difficulties or rain and wind*
precious	*something important to you*
to lead	*to show someone the way*
pregnant	*expecting a child*
weak	*not strong*
desolate	*troubled / not knowing what to do*
to combine	*to put things together*
an experience	*something that happens to you*

PAGE 26   ANSWERS TO THE WORKBOOK QUESTIONS   EXERCISE 2:

1. What does Ethan do?

   Ethan sings in the church.

2. **What is important to him?**
   The church is important to him.
3. **What gives him strength and hope?**
   The church gives him strength and hope.
4. **How does he help the church?**
   He sings for the church.
5. **Why can't the church pay him more money?**
   The church is poor.
6. **Why does he need more money?**
   He needs to have enough for his family to live on.
7. **What has he always studied?**
   He has always studied singing.
8. **Are most churches very poor?**
   No, not all churches are poor.
   Some churches are poor.

PAGE 27   ANSWERS TO THE WORKBOOK QUESTIONS   EXERCISE 3:

Ethan **was** a gospel singer. The church **was** very important to him because it **gave** him strength and hope. He **wanted** to help support the church with his singing but many churches **were** poor. They **weren't** able to pay him enough money for his wife and two children to live on. He **had** only studied singing.

Teacher Guide

LESSON 12 REVIEW

ORAL QUESTIONS

Are you a singer?	Yes, I'm a singer.
	No, I'm not a singer.
Did you ever meet an alien from space?	Yes, I met an alien from space.
	No, I haven't ever met an alien from space.
Did you ever record something?	Yes, I recorded something.
	No, I didn't ever record anything.
You don't usually give up, do you?	Yes, I sometimes give up.
	No, I don't usually give up.
Do popular artists have a lot of fans?	Yes, popular artists have a lot of fans.
Was there a rock concert here last weekend?	Yes, there was a rock concert here last weekend.
	No, there wasn't a rock concert here last…
Do people sing gospel songs in churches? Do you often watch videos?	Yes, people sing gospel songs in churches.
	Yes, I often watch videos.
	No, I don't often watch videos.
	No, I never watch videos.
Do your friends record music?	Yes, my friends record music.
	No, my friends don't record music.
Do you enjoy big changes in your life?	Yes, I enjoy big changes in my life.
	No, I don't enjoy big changes in my life.
Do you read a lot of books?	Yes, I read a lot of books.
	No, I don't read a lot of books.
Do you know a lot of songs?	Yes, I know a lot of songs.
	No, I don't know a lot of songs.
Is music important to you?	Yes, music is important to me.
	No, music isn't important to me.
Did you ever injure yourself?	Yes, I've injured myself.
	No, I haven't ever injured myself.
Do you listen to much music?	Yes, I listen to a lot of music.
	No, I don't listen to much music.
	No, I don't listen to a lot of music.
Do you have much time for sports?	Yes, I have a lot of time for sports.
	No, I don't have much time for sports.
	No, I don't have a lot of time for sports.
Do most people have problems?	Yes, most people have problems.
Do you think the rich people have problems?	Yes, I think the rich people have problems.
	No, I don't think the rich people have problems.
Have you ever been out in a storm?	Yes, I've been out in a storm.
	No, I haven't ever been out in a storm.
Do you combine working and studying?	Yes, I combine working and studying.
	No, I don't combine working and studying.

Teacher Guide

LESSON 12 CONTINUED

PAGE 29 **ANSWERS TO THE WORKBOOK QUESTIONS** **EXERCISE 1:**

1. Thousands of people listen to **_gospel music._**
   Thousands **_of people listen to it_**.
2. Sometimes it's very difficult to solve **_problems._**
   Sometimes **_it's very difficult to solve them_**.
3. One of the most beautiful gospel songs was written by **_Thomas Dorsey._**
   One of the most **_beautiful gospel songs was written by him_**.
4. Jack Scott pitched for the **_fans_**.
   Jack Scott **_pitched for them_**.

PAGE 29 **ANSWERS TO THE WORKBOOK QUESTIONS** **EXERCISE 2:**

1. I like listening to music, **_so_** I have many CD's.
2. The Negro people are very musical **_so_** they write their own songs.
3. People can sing in church **_but_** / **_and_** they can sing at home, too.
4. Thomas Dorsey was very sad **_so_** he started playing the piano.
5. The words and music that Dorsey wrote are very beautiful **_so_** / **_and_** everyone enjoys them.
6. Mahalia Jackson sang gospel music on the radio **_and_** / **_but_** she often sang it in churches, too.

PAGE 30 **ANSWERS TO THE CROSSWORD PUZZLE** **EXERCISE 3:**

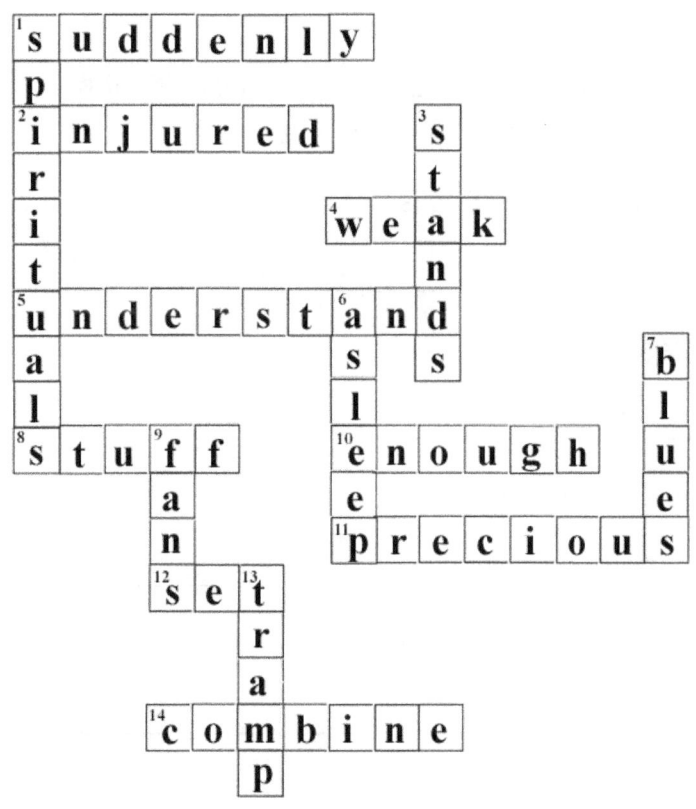

Teacher Guide

LESSONS 9 TO 12   TEST 3   NAME: _____

Answer these questions in sentences. (4 marks each)

1. _____
2. _____
3. _____
4. _____
5. _____

Use object pronouns instead of the underlined word. (2 marks each)

6. This <u>music</u> is very relaxing. Do you like _____.

7. Did you see our <u>friends</u>? Yes, I saw _____.

Write one of these joining words on the line between the clauses. (2 marks each)

but or so

8. Thomas Dorsey was very sad _____ he started playing the piano.

9. I like listening to jazz _____ I like other kinds of music, too.

10. Tommy Dorsey could play blues, jazz _____ gospel music.

Answer these questions in sentences. (4 marks each)

11. Do you study computers as well as English?

    _____

12. Does jazz make you feel good?

    _____

13. Do you think there are aliens in space?

    _____

14. Are there many churches in your country?

    _____

15. Did you get enough to eat yesterday?

    _____

LESSON 12 CONTINUED

ORAL QUESTIONS FOR TEST 3 (4 marks each)
1. Do you think sports are important?
2. Do you read a lot of books?
3. Do popular singers have a lot of fans?
4. Do you listen to much music?
5. You don't usually give up, do you?

ANSWERS FOR TEST 3
1. Yes, I think sports are important.
   No, I don't think sports are important.
2. Yes, I read a lot of books.
   No, I don't read a lot of books.
3. Yes, popular singers have a lot of fans.
4. Yes, I listen to a lot of music.
   No, I don't listen to much music.
   No, I don't listen to a lot of music.
5. Yes, I sometimes give up.
   No, I don't usually give up.

6. This music is very relaxing. Do you like _**it**_? (2 marks each)
7. Did you see our friends? Yes, I saw _**them**_.

Write one of these joining words on the line between the clauses. (2 marks each)
but or so
8. Thomas Dorsey was very sad _**so**_ he started playing the piano.
9. I like listening to jazz _**but**_ I like other kinds of music, too.
10. Tommy Dorsey could play blues, jazz _**or**_ gospel music.

Answer these questions in sentences. (4 marks each)
11. **Do you study computers as well as English?** Yes, I study computers as well as English. No, I don't study computers as well as English.
12. **Does jazz make you feel good?**
    Yes, jazz makes me feel good.
    No, jazz doesn't make me feel good.
13. **Do you think there are aliens in space?**
    Yes, I think there are aliens in space.
    No, I don't think there are aliens in space.
14. **Are there many churches in our country?** Yes, there are many churches in our country. No, there aren't many churches in our country.
15. **Did you get enough to eat yesterday?**
    Yes, I got enough to eat yesterday.
    No, I didn't get enough to eat yesterday.

Teacher Guide

LESSON 13
ORAL QUESTIONS

Did you get up early this morning?	Yes, I got up early this morning.
	No, I didn't get up early this morning.
Does this country have a royal family?	Yes, this country has a royal family.
	No, this country doesn't have a royal family.
Did Queen Victoria influence the moral code of the people?	Yes, she influenced the moral code of the people.
Where were the men supposed to be in the evenings?	They were supposed to be at home.
What kind of clothes should the women wear?	The women should wear clothes that covered them from their shoulders to their ankles.
Was it acceptable for a man to touch a woman?	No, it was not acceptable for a man to touch a woman.
Was it acceptable for a man to kiss a woman's hand?	Yes, it was acceptable for a man to kiss a woman's hand.
Did all people follow Queen Victoria's moral code?	No, many people just pretended to follow it.
Were unmarried women with babies accepted?	No, unmarried women with babies were not accepted.
Did the unmarried women with babies suffer?	Yes, the unmarried women with babies did suffer.
Do you think Queen Victoria set a good example?	Yes, she set a good example.
	No, she didn't set a good example.
Can single mothers get a good job today?	Yes, single mothers can get a good job today.
Do you think the leaders of countries should set a good example?	Yes, I think the leaders of countries should set a good example.
Do many people live in poverty?	Yes, many people live in poverty.
Do all countries have problems to solve?	Yes, all countries have problems to solve.
Is there a group that sets the moral code here?	Yes, there is a group of people that sets the moral code here.
	No, there isn't a group of people that sets the...

Teacher Guide

LESSON 13 CONTINUED

PAGE 31   ANSWERS TO THE WORKBOOK QUESTIONS   EXERCISE 1:

to influence	to get people to think as you do
a century	100 years
to set an example	to teach something by doing it
social behavior	what people do
to pretend	actors do it well
to touch	to put your hand on something
poverty	no money/poor
to be acceptable	to do what your culture says is correct

PAGE 31   ANSWERS TO THE WORKBOOK QUESTIONS   EXERCISE 2:

1. The Royal Family was the social leader of the British Empire.
2. Queen Victoria changed the moral code of the British Empire.
3. Men were expected to be at home with their families every night.
4. Women were to wear clothes that covered them from their shoulders to their ankles.
5. No, some people only pretended to follow her moral code.
6. The women suffered the most from her moral code.

PAGE 32   POSSIBLE ANSWERS TO THE WORKBOOK QUESTIONS   EXERCISE 3:

1. Some people **just pretended** to follow Queen Victoria's moral code.
2. Queen Victoria influenced England as well as **the rest of** the British Empire.

PAGE 32   ANSWERS TO THE WORKBOOK QUESTIONS   EXERCISE 4:

baby – **babies**	opportunity – **opportunities**
society – **societies**	party – **parties**

PAGE 32   POSSIBLE ANSWERS TO THE WORKBOOK QUESTIONS   EXERCISE 5:

1. Queen Victoria influenced the moral code of her times **but her influence didn't reach this country. /on the other hand she didn't help the poor.**
2. The Royal family was the social leader **but many people just pretended to follow it. / on the other hand, only the rich counted.**
3. Men were expected to be at home with their families each evening, **but in our country… / on the other hand they were often out with their friends.**
4. Women were to wear clothes that covered their bodies **whereas in our country…**
5. Illegitimate children couldn't get good jobs when they became adults, **whereas …**

Teacher Guide

LESSON 13 CONTINUED

PAGE 33   POSSIBLE ANSWERS TO THE WORKBOOK QUESTIONS   EXERCISE 6:

Note to the teacher:
Numbers 1 to 4 are interchangeable.
Numbers 5 and 7 are interchangeable
but the verb *like* must be followed by the infinitive *to*…

1. I **must** meet my friend a 9:00 PM.
2. I **have to** pay the restaurant bill.
3. I **had to** go to work / get more exercise.
4. I **have got to** go to English class.
5. I **will** go to the club
6. I am **going to** have lunch / catch a bus.
7. I **would like to** become a rock star.
8. We **must** go to English class/ listen more carefully.
9. They **have to** go to work.
10. Most people **would like to** make a lot of money.

ACTIVITY 5:
Divide into groups of three or four.
Make a conversation, write it down, and be prepared to present it to the class.
The time is during Queen Victoria's reign. The conversation is between three or four people.

MARILYN
Marilyn thinks the queen's moral code is a good thing.

ROBERT
Robert, Marilyn's husband thinks the ladies' clothes must be very uncomfortable, and restricts their movement and breathing.

WILLIAM
William, their son, doesn't think any of it is practical, and people should act the way they want to.

SALLY
Sally is their daughter. She finds that the women's clothing is very difficult. The long skirts get wet and muddy outside, and the waists are so tight it restricts her breathing.

Teacher Guide

LESSON 14
ORAL QUESTIONS

Who was Edward VII?
Where did Edward VII and his wife travel? Was it a good time for parties?

*Edward VII was the oldest son of Queen Victoria. They traveled through Europe.
Yes, it was a good time for parties.*

What kind of clothes did the rich wear?
Was the British Empire strong at that time? Were Edward and his wife well liked?

*They wore beautiful clothes.
Yes, the British Empire was very strong.
Yes, they were very well liked.*

Were the women able to vote at that time?
How often do you vote?
What did the suffragettes want?

*No, the women were not able to vote.
I vote _____.
They wanted to be able to vote.*

Why was it called the "Age of Men"?

It was called the "Age of Men" because the men had all the power.

Why couldn't Edward become king when he was younger?

He couldn't become king until his mother died.

Would you like to travel throughout Europe?

*Yes, I'd like to travel throughout Europe.
No, I wouldn't like to travel throughout Europe. Yes, I'd want to travel in spite of a war.*

Would you want to travel in spite of a war?

*No, I wouldn't want to travel in spite of war.
Yes, rich people have a lot of power.*

Do rich people have much power?

Did you ever go to a theater?

*Yes, I went to a theater.
No, I didn't ever go to a theater.
Yes, I spend a lot of time at the theater.
No, I don't spend much time at the theater.
Yes, everyone can vote in our country.*

Do you spend much time at the theater?

Can everyone vote in our country?

How many men are here?

*There are _____ men here.
There aren't any men here.
Yes, he waited for the death of his mother.
Yes, there was a depression in this country.
No, there wasn't a depression in this country.*

Did Edward wait for the death of his mother? Was there a depression in this country?

Does anyone in this country wear a crown? Was there ever a war in our country?

*Yes, _____ wears a crown.
No, no one wears a crown.
Yes, there was a war in our country.
No, there wasn't ever a war in our country.
Yes, rich people have a lot of money.
Yes, there is plenty of food in our country.
No, there isn't plenty of food in our country.*

Do rich people have a lot of money?
Is there plenty of food in our country?

Teacher Guide

LESSON 14 CONTINUED

PAGE 34 **ANSWERS TO THE WORKBOOK QUESTIONS** **EXERCISE 1:**

1. Whose son was Edward?
   Edward was Queen Victoria's son.
2. Before he was crowned, how did Edward spend his time? *He spent his time visiting friends.*
3. What did the rich people do while Edward was king?
   They went to a lot of parties.
4. Who had all the power within British society?
   The men had all the power.
5. Who tried to stop the men?
   The suffragettes tried to stop the men.

PAGE 34 **ANSWERS TO MATCH THE MEANING** **EXERCISE 2:**

well known	someone everyone knows
plenty	a lot
power	you can *make people do what you want*
suffragettes	women who wanted to vote
the depression (1930's)	a time when business was bad, people were hungry even though
in spite of	
rich	people with a lot of money
bored	not having enough to think about or do
to crown	to make a person king or queen
to attend	to go to

PAGE 35 **ANSWERS TO THE WORKBOOK QUESTIONS** **EXERCISE 3:**

1. Edward was 60 years old when he was crowned king.
2. It was a good time for the rich. / There were parties, and dances.
3. The people liked Edward VII.
4. Rich men had all the power.
5. The first war, the depression, and the second war made the times difficult.
6. Yes, I'd want to live during the "Age of Men".
   No, I wouldn't want to live during the "Age of Men".

PAGE 35 ANSWERS TO THE WORKBOOK QUESTIONS
    EXERCISE 4:

1. Edward, **who** became king at age 60, only ruled the British Empire for eight years.
2. The suffragettes, **who** fought for the vote, wanted some of the power.
3. Edward, **who** couldn't become king until his mother died, had a good time in Europe. Edward, **who** had a good time, couldn't become king until his mother died.
4. The Suffragettes, **who** wanted to be able to vote, wanted some of the power.

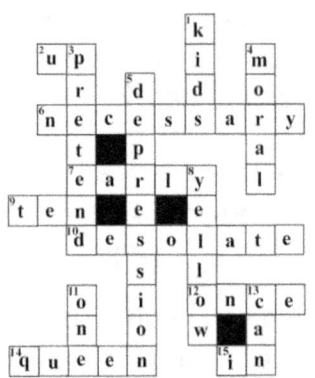

PAGE 36 ANSWER TO THE CROSSWORD PUZZLE

Teacher Guide

LESSON 15

ORAL QUESTIONS

How old was Edward VIII when he became king? Did the English people love their king? Did the people want Edward to marry Wallis?	*Edward VIII was 42 when he became king. Yes, they loved their king.* *No, they didn't want Edward to marry her.*
Was he interested in government? Who was his lover? Was Wallis Simpson British?	*No, he wasn't interested in government. Wallis Warfield Simpson was his lover.* *No, she was American.* *No, she wasn't British.*
Was Wallis Simpson divorced? Could the king marry a divorced American? What did Edward VIII do?	*Yes, she was divorced.* *No, the king couldn't marry a divorced American.* *Edward VIII gave up the throne of England.*
Did Edward VIII marry Wallis Simpson? Could the royal family accept her?	*Yes, he married Wallace Simpson.* *No, the royal family couldn't accept her.*
Did Edward live in England after he married her?	*No, he lived in France.*
Who became king of England after Edward VIII? Do you think Edward was right to marry for love?	*Edward's brother George became king. Yes, he was right to marry for love.* *No, he wasn't right to marry for love.*
What would you do if you were Edward?	*If I were Edward, I would _____.*
Did the other members of the royal family forgive Edward? Would you like to be king / queen?	*No, they never forgave him.* *Yes, I'd like to be king / queen.* *No, I wouldn't like to be king / queen.*
Is the Royal family part of Britain's upper class?	*Yes, they are part of Britain's upper class.*
Are there upper class people in our country?	*Yes, there are upper class people here.* *No, there aren't any upper class people…*
Was the British Empire very large? What do you buy in a pub? Do we have pubs here? Do you vote for the people in your government?	*Yes, it was very large.* *I buy whisky, beer or wine.* *Yes, we have pubs.* *No, we don't have pubs.* *Yes, we vote for the people in our government.*
Do many people live alone?	*Yes, many people live alone.*
Is a mall a street? Will you marry your heart's desire?	*Yes, a mall is a street.* *Yes, I'll marry my heart's desire.* *I'm already married.*

Teacher Guide

LESSON 15 CONTINUED

PAGE 37   **ANSWERS TO THE WORKBOOK QUESTIONS**   **EXERCISE 1:**

1. What kind of a man was Edward?
   He was a party loving man.
2. Was he interested in government?
   No, he was not interested in government.
3. Why couldn't Wallis become queen?
   She was a divorced American.
4. How did Edward solve his problem?
   He gave up his (right to the) throne.

PAGE 37   **ANSWERS TO MATCH THE MEANING**   **EXERCISE 2:**

to fall in love in spite of	*in a short time you have a strong love for someone even though*
his heart's desire	*what he wanted the most*
to forgive	*to pardon*
a violin	*it's a musical instrument*

Sentences using: to decide, to pretend, to want

PAGE 37   **SAMPLE SENTENCES:**   **EXERCISE 3**

1. We decided to go home early.

2. The man pretended to help.

3. The children really wanted to go to the theatre.

PAGE 38 SUGGESTED ANSWERS TO THE WORKBOOK QUESTIONS ACTIVITY 3:

Narrator: A number of weeks later, Edward told the British people that he would marry Wallis Simpson. The people said they would never accept a divorced American as their queen. Edward and Wallis are alone. They plan their future.
Edward: Nothing will come between us.
Wallis: The people will never **_accept me as queen._**
Edward: You are right but **_I will think of something._**
Wallis: How can you?
Edward: If I give up my **_throne_**.
Wallis: Would you be happy?
Edward: Oh yes, my love. We will go **_to France_**.
Wallis: But you are king of the **_British Empire_**.
Edward: You are the most important to me. We will have parties and **_go to the theater_**.

Teacher Guide

LESSON 15 CONTINUED

PAGE 31 — **ANSWERS TO THE STUDENT BOOK QUESTIONS ACTIVITY 4:**
The following are adverbs that could be used. Others are possible.

1. The queen *frequently* goes to London.
2. The British people *mostly* love their royalty.
3. A lot of tourists *always* go to Buckingham Palace.
4. The queen *never* cooks dinner.
5. The Royal Family *generally* sets an example.
6. Edward VIII *often* went to parties.
7. The queen *frequently* visits other countries
8. The Royal Family *never* forgave Edward.
9. Queen Victoria *always* wore long dresses.
10. King Edward VII *often* danced in spite of the shadows of war.
11. Edward VIII *always* loved Wallis Warfield Simpson.
12. Queen Victoria *never* liked to run.

PAGE 31 — **ANSWERS TO THE STUDENT BOOK QUESTIONS ACTIVITY 5:**

1. The girl walked home.
   The girl walked home by herself.
2. The boy wrote the best paragraph.
   The boy wrote the best paragraph by himself.
3. You must solve the problem.
   You must solve the problem (by) yourself.
4. We really need to study.
   We really need to study by ourselves.
5. They cleaned the room.
   They cleaned the room by themselves.
6. The dog was at home.
   The dog was at home by itself.

PAGE 37 — **WORKBOOK QUESTIONS** — **EXERCISE 3:**

NOTE TO THE TEACHER:
Please check to be sure that the student's sentences are correct.

Tell the students it is important that they memorize the sentences they have written **or** the ones used in the example. This is the best way for them to learn which verbs are followed by infinitives.

They will be asked to write the sentences they have learned in future assignments.

PAGES 38, 39 AND 40   ANSWERS TO THE WORKBOOK QUESTIONS ACTIVITY 7:

He was alone, so he worked on the car himself.   **The children played on the beach by themselves.**   **Evelyn's mother lives by herself.**

Teacher Guide

LESSON 15 CONTINUED

Edward and Wallis didn't want the crown for themselves.

The British thought themselves the best.

Buckingham Palace stands by itself at the end of a long mall.

He runs by himself.

Do you listen to music when you are by yourself?

Queen Victoria saw herself as the best queen.

I can play the violin by myself.

Queen Victoria sometimes cooked dinner by herself.

She went shopping by herself.

He ate the whole pizza himself.

The musical group practiced by itself.

The dog was at home by itself.

LESSON 15 CONTINUED

ACTIVITY 5: SENTENCES FOR THE STUDENTS

1. He was alone, so he worked on the car by himself.

2. The children on the beach played by themselves.

3. Evelyn's mother lives by herself.

4. Edward and Wallis didn't want the crown for themselves.

5. The British thought themselves the best.

6. Buckingham Palace stands by itself at the end of a long mall.

7. He runs by himself.

8. Do you listen to music when you are by yourself?

9. Queen Victoria saw herself as the best queen.

10. I can play the violin by myself.

11. Queen Victoria sometimes cooked dinner herself.

12. She went shopping by herself.

13. He ate the whole pizza himself.

14. The musical group practiced by itself.

15. The dog was at home by itself.

LESSON 16

ORAL QUESTIONS

Did Queen Victoria influence the moral code? *Yes, she influenced the moral code*

Could unmarried women with a baby get a good job? *No, unmarried women with a baby couldn't get a good job.*

Is today's moral code the same as Victoria's? *No, it's not the same as Victoria's*

Why didn't Edward stay the king of England? *He married against the people's wishes.*

What did the Suffragettes want?

Did some people just pretend to follow Queen Victoria's moral code? *Yes, some people just pretended to follow her moral code.*

Are you interested in what famous people do? *Yes, I'm interested in what famous people do.*
No, I'm not interested in what famous people do.

Is there much poverty in this country? *Yes, there is a lot of poverty in this country. No, there isn't much poverty in this country.*

Do many poor people suffer? *Yes, many poor people suffer.*

Do our country's leaders set a good example? *Yes, they set a good example.*
No, they don't set a good example.

Do you belong to a group? *Yes, I belong to a group.*
No, I don't belong to a group.

Do you spend much money on food? *Yes, I spend a lot of money on food.*
No, I don't spend much money on food.

Is this a new century? *Yes, this is a new century.*
No, this is not a new country.

Would you give up your true love to be king? *Yes, I'd give up my true love to be king.*
No, I wouldn't give up my true love to be king.

Did you clean your home today? *Yes, I cleaned my home today.*
No, I didn't clean my home today.

Does our government have a lot of power? *Yes, our government has a lot of power.*
No, our government doesn't have a lot of power.
No, our government doesn't have much power.

Are there many rich people in our country? *Yes, there are a lot of rich people.*
No, there aren't a lot of rich people.
No, there aren't many rich people.

When did you get up this morning? *I got up at _____ (o'clock / AM)*

Teacher Guide

LESSON 16 CONTINUED

PAGE 41 ANSWERS TO THE WORKBOOKBOOK QUESTIONS   EXERCISE 1:

1. moral, the, Queen Victoria, of, Empire, the, influenced, code, British
   Queen Victoria influenced the moral code of the British Empire.
2. gave, kingdom, for, Edward, Wallis, a, up
   Edward gave up his kingdom for Wallis.
3. twentieth, The, of, beginning, was, the, "Age of men", the, century
   The beginning of the twentieth century was the "Age of Men".
4. wanted, The, to, able, be, to, suffragettes, vote
   The suffragettes wanted to be able to vote.

Page 41   ANSWERS TO THE WORKBOOK QUESTIONS   EXERCISE 2:

1. **Poor people** suffer from hunger if no one helps *them*.
2. Edward VIII loved Wallis **Simpson**. He married *her*.
3. Bill bought a **new car** last week. Did you see *it*?
4. She has some **new books**. Did you see *them*?
5. We saw the people there, but they didn't talk to **us**. Did they talk to *you*?

PAGE 42   ANSWERS TO THE CROSSWORD PUZZLE EXERCISE 4:

Teacher Guide

LESSON 15 CONTINUED

TEST 4   ORAL QUESTIONS

QUESTIONS	ANSWERS
1. Is there much poverty in our country?	Yes, there is a lot of poverty in our country.
2. Do you ever talk about government?	Yes, I talk about government.
	No, I don't talk about government.
3. Do you spend much money?	Yes, I spend a lot of money.
	No, I don't spend much money.
4. Do you belong to a group?	Yes, I belong to a group.
	No, I don't belong to a group.
5. Do rich people have a lot of influence?	Yes, rich people have a lot of influence.
	No, rich people don't have a lot of influence.
6. Is this the twentieth century?	No, it's not the twentieth century.

ANSWERS TO THE TEST QUESTIONS

7. During the "Age of Men" all the men enjoyed **_themselves_**.
8. The dog stayed at home by **_itself_**.
9. We don't have to live like Queen Victoria, so we can enjoy **_ourselves_**.

Queen Victoria 10 **_influenced_** the way people thought. Men could not 11 **_touch_** a lady. A woman's clothes covered her 12 **_body_** from her 13 **_shoulders_** to her 14 **_ankles_**. She
thought that men should be 15 **_at home_** in the evenings. Not everyone followed Victoria's moral code. Some people only 16 **_pretended_** to follow it.

17. Do you sometimes go to parties?
     Yes, I often go to parties. / No, I (seldom, never) go to parties.
18. Do our country's leaders set a good example?
     Yes, they set a good example. / No, they don't set a good example.
19. Do people suffer when they are hungry?
     Yes, people suffer when they are hungry.
20. Would you have married Wallis Simpson if you were Edward VIII? Yes, I would have married her. / No I wouldn't have married her.

LESSONS 13 TO 16   TEST 4   NAME _____

Answer the oral questions in sentences. (4 marks each)

1. _____
2. _____
3. _____
4. _____
5. _____
6. _____

Complete the sentences using some of the following: (1 mark each)

myself, yourself, himself, herself, itself,   ourselves, yourselves, themselves

7. During the "Age of Men" all the men enjoyed _____.

8. The dog stayed at home by _____.

9. We don't have to live like Queen Victoria, so we can enjoy _____.

Fill in the blanks using the words below. (1 mark each)

| pretended | body | century | shoulders |
| ankles | influenced | at home | touch |

Queen Victoria 10 _____ the way people thought. Men could not 11 _____ a lady.

A woman's clothes covered her 12 _____ from her 13 _____ to her 14 _____.

She thought that men should be 15 _____ in the evenings. Not everyone followed Victoria's moral code. Some people only 16 _____ to follow it.

Answer in sentences. (4 marks each)

17. Do you sometimes go to parties?

_____

18. Do our country's leaders set a good example?

_____

19. Do people suffer when they are hungry?

_____

20. If you were Edward VIII, would you marry Wallis Simpson?

_____

Teacher Guide

ORAL QUESTIONS FOR TEST 5
Answer these questions in sentences (4 marks each)

1. Will you be taking a bus tomorrow?
   Yes, I'll be taking a bus tomorrow.
   No, I won't be taking a bus tomorrow.

2. Have you ever driven a truck?
   Yes, I've driven a truck.
   No, I haven't ever driven a truck.

3. Are you going to be at work tomorrow?
   Yes, I'm going to be at work tomorrow.
   No, I'm not going to be at work tomorrow.

4. Do you spend much time at the theater?
   Yes, I spend a lot of time at the theater.
   No, I don't spend much time at the theater.

5. Do you enjoy changes in your life?
   Yes, I enjoy changes in my life.
   No, I don't enjoy changes in my life.

6. Do rich people have much influence?
   Yes, rich people have a lot of influence.
   No, rich people don't have very much influence.

7. Have you lived here for a long time?
   Yes, I have lived here for a long time.
   No, I haven't lived here for a long time.

8. Do all countries have problems?
   Yes, all countries have problems.

9. Did you get enough sleep last night?
   Yes, I got enough sleep last night.
   No, I didn't get enough sleep last night.

10. Are you going to be visiting your friend tonight?
    Yes, I'm going to be visiting my friend tonight.
    No, I'm not going to be visiting my friend tonight.

Read the paragraphs and answer the questions in sentences, (4 marks each).

11. Who was like a dark shadow throughout Diana's marriage?
    Camilla Parker-Bowles was like a dark shadow throughout Diana's marriage.

12. What made Diana sick?
    Her unhappiness made her sick.

13. Why did she think she wasn't as good as the others in the royal family?
    She thought she wasn't as good as the others because she couldn't please them. She couldn't please them. (Give 3 marks)

14. What helped her to become strong?
    The British people helped her to become strong.

Teacher Guide

ANSWERS TO TEST 5 QUESTIONS
Complete these sentences using object pronouns instead of the underlined word. (2 marks each)

16. Will you be wearing your hat tomorrow? Yes, I'll be wearing *it*.
17. Will you see your friends soon? No, I won't see **them**.
18. Are visitors coming to talk to our class today? Yes, they're coming to talk to **us**.

19. Did you see a picture of Princess Diana? Yes, I saw a picture of **her**.

20. Was that your picture in the newspaper? Yes, it was a picture of **me**.
21. Charles was talking on TV. Did you see **him**?

Put the verbs into the correct tense. (4 marks each)

Ever since Diana's death the British people (22) (to miss) **have missed** her.
They were always interested in what she did each day. For the past few years, pictures of her two boys (23) (to be) **have been** in the newspapers.
The people (24) (to watch) **have watched** them grow ever since they were born.
For many years the British people (25) (to be) **have been** proud of them.

Join these sentences using: but, or, so (3 marks each)

26. Electric cars don't pollute the air, **so** they are becoming popular.
27. Lady Gaga went to university **but** university life didn't suit her.
28. Lady Gaga was criticized because she empowered women and gay people **but** her mother taught her to be tolerant.
29. You might like Lady Gaga, **or** you might prefer other performers.

LESSONS 1 TO 20 TEST 5 NAME: _____

Answer these questions in sentences. (4 marks each)

1. _____
2. _____
3. _____
4. _____
5. _____
6. _____
7. _____
8. _____
9. _____
10. _____

Read the paragraphs and answer the questions in sentences. (4 marks each)

Camilla Parker-Bowles was like a dark shadow throughout Diana's marriage. There were three people in their marriage.

Her unhappiness made her sick with bulimia. She thought she wasn't as good as the others in the royal family because she couldn't please them.

When she found that the British people loved her, she became stronger and started to use her position to help thousands of people throughout the world.

11. Who was a dark shadow throughout Diana's marriage?

    _____

12. What made Diana sick?

    _____

13. Why did she think she wasn't as good as the others in the royal family?

    _____

14. What helped her to become strong?

    _____

Teacher Guide

LESSON 20 CONTINUED

Complete these sentences using object pronouns instead of the underlined word. (2marks each)

16. Will you be wearing your hat tomorrow? Yes, I'll be wearing _____.

17. Will you see your friends soon? No, I won't see _____.

18. Are visitors coming to our class today? Yes, they're coming to talk to _____.

19. Did you see a picture of Princess Diana? Yes, I saw a picture of _____.

20. Was that your picture in the paper? Yes, it was a picture of _____.

21. Charles was talking on TV. Did you see _____?

Put the verbs into the correct tense. (4 marks each)

Ever since Diana's death the British people (22) (to miss)

_____ her. They were always interested in what she did each

day. For the past few years, pictures of her

two boys (23) (to be) _____ in the newspapers.

The people (24) (to watch) _____ them grow ever since they

were born. For many years the British people (25) (to be)

Join these sentences using: but, or, so (3 marks each)
_____ proud of them.

26. Electric cars don't pollute the air. They are becoming popular.
_____

27. Lady Gaga went to university. University life didn't suit her.
_____

28. Lady Gaga was criticized because she empowered women and gay people. Her mother taught her to be tolerant.
_____

29. You might like Lady Gaga. You might prefer other performers.
_____

Teacher Guide

The History of Flight

Intermediate to Advanced ESL Lesson plans

20 ESL Lesson Plans for Intermediate to Advanced Students

Includes:

- Full downloadable Audio
- Student Worksheets
- Teacher Guide

Learning English Curriculum

Since 1999

www.efl-esl.com

Includes Full Audio

Lesson 1

VOCABULARY

fascinate (to)
eagle
kingdom
wing

forth
snake
mythology
throne
righteousness

dragon
heal, to
heel
shine, to
symbol

ACTIVITY 1: Listen to your teacher and or the sound file read the paragraphs, then take turns reading the paragraphs orally.

https://tinyurl.com/2wtn45a9

Have you ever looked at the sky? People are always fascinated with the sky. It changes from minute to minute.

Since very early times, people have watched the birds flying high above their heads. Mythology is full of stories about flying. Mercury was said to be the messenger of the gods. It was said that he had little wings on his hat and heels so he could travel very quickly.

One emperor in Persia was said to have a beautiful throne, and he had eagles that would lift him and his throne high into the sky so that he could see all parts of his kingdom.

Certainly, we know that flight was thought about a lot by people in ancient times. One of the earliest symbols to be found in Egypt is the winged sun. It had an important part in their religion.

Pegasus the flying horse

Hundreds of years later this symbol was used in the early writings of the Jewish people, and later the same sentence is found in the Bible: "the sun of righteousness will certainly shine forth, with healing in his wings."

Everywhere you look in ancient mythology, you will find creatures that fly. There are flying snakes, flying dragons and all kinds of flying creatures.

The Greeks even had a flying horse called Pegasus.

ORAL QUESTIONS TEACHER'S GUIDE

History of Flight - Student Reader

Lesson 1 Continued

ACTIVITY 2: Divide into small groups. Answer these questions. Then check your answers.

1. Do you ever wish you could fly like a bird?
2. Who was Mercury?
3. How was Mercury able to move quickly?
4. What was Pegasus?
5. Were flying creatures to be found in ancient mythology?

1. Yes, I sometimes wish I could fly like a bird. No, I don't ever wish I could fly like a bird.
2. Mercury was the messenger of the gods.
3. Mercury had wings on his heels and on his hat.
4. Pegasus was a flying horse.
5. Yes, there were many flying creatures in ancient mythology.

EXERCISE 1 - Workbook page 1
ACTIVITY 3 – Workbook page 1

GERUNDS
A gerund is the – ing form of the verb. It is used as a noun.
It is used in the same way as a noun – as a subject of an object.
Gerunds are used in sentences in three ways:

1. The subject of a sentence:
<u>Flying</u> through the air would be fun.

2. The object of a verb:
I love <u>flying</u>.

3. The object of a preposition:
The birds were tired from <u>flying</u>.

ACTIVITY 3: Divide into small groups. Answer these questions using gerunds for the verb given.

1. Pegasus enjoyed (to fly).
2. Flying can be faster than (to run).
3. Mercury was famous for (to move) quickly.
4. (to fly) creatures were common in mythology.
5. Dragons had wings for (to fly).
6. Early people were fascinated with (to fly).
7. (to fly) is very common today.
8. (to read) about ancient times is interesting.
9. (to find) things to read about in ancient mythology is easy.
10. He always watched the birds (to fly).

1. Pegasus enjoyed flying.
2. Flying can be faster than running.
3. Mercury was famous for moving quickly.
4. Flying creatures were common in mythology.
5. Dragons had wings for flying.
6. Early people were fascinated with flying.
7. Flying is very common today.
8. Reading about ancient times is interesting.
9. Finding things to read about in ancient mythology is easy.
10. He always watched the birds flying.

EXERCISE 2 - Workbook page 2

Lesson 2

VOCABULARY

myth	maze	puzzle	garden
bush escape,	design, to	hide, to	prison
to fall apart, to	feather	wax	melt, to
push, to	sea	teach, to	nephew
remember, to	tower	partridge	goddess

ACTIVITY 1 : Listen to the audio and your teacher read the passage, then take turns reading the paragraphs orally.

Don't try to fly too high!

There is a myth from ancient Greece that talks about flying.

There was a man called Dāedalus who was very smart. The king asked him to make a maze. This is like a giant puzzle, made so that once you are inside, you will never be able to find your way out again. Today, some say that this maze was a huge building with hundreds of halls. However, mostly people believe that it was a huge garden, with rows of bushes, and designed to hide the way out.

After it was finished, the king put Daedalus and his son Ĭcarus in prison. Daedalus watched the birds, and decided that flying would be the only way for them to escape. He made two big wings for himself, using feathers and wax. When he tried the new wings, he found that he could fly like a bird. He made a second pair of wings and gave them to Icarus. He taught Icarus how to fly.

Just before they escaped he told Icarus that he mustn't fly too high. He said that the sun would melt the wax and his wings would fall apart.

Lesson 2 Continued

Icarus was a young boy, and he loved flying. He didn't listen to his father and flew very high, close to the sun. The sun melted his wings, and Icarus fell into the sea and died.

Later, Daedalus was living in the palace of another king. Because he was very smart, he made many new things. He was asked to teach the king's nephew, Perdix, how to make things. Soon Daedalus found that Perdix was smarter than he was.

One day, Daedalus pushed Perdix off a high tower. Minerva the goddess saw this. She didn't want him to die, so she changed him into a partridge. The partridge flew safely to the ground. Today everyone knows that partridges don't fly into high places and they make their nests on the ground. It is said they still remember, and are afraid to fly too high.

EXERCISE 1: Workbook page 3

ORAL QUESTIONS TEACHER'S GUIDE
Role-play this conversation with your teacher,
ACTIVITY 2: then role-play it in small groups.

Narrator:	The two friends are talking about Daedalus and Icarus. This story shows that even people a long time ago thought about flying.
Paul:	Well, it was a great way to get away from the king!
Julia:	It wasn't so great for Icarus. He fell into the sea!
Paul:	That was because he didn't listen to his father.
Julia:	Young boys don't like to listen to their fathers.
Paul:	Maybe that's why the story is remembered.
Julia:	It was meant to teach a lesson.
Paul:	I think you're right, Julia.

EXERCISE 2: Workbook page 3
EXERCISE 3: Workbook page 4

Lesson 2 Continued

ACTIVITY 2 : Divide into small groups.
Ask each other the questions, then check your answers.

1. What did Mercury do?
2. How did the Persian emperor see his kingdom?
3. Were there flying creatures in ancient mythology?
4. What was the name of the flying horse?
5. Do you think flying would be fun?
6. Were early people fascinated with flying?
7. Why did Daedalus make wings?
8. What were the wings made of?
9. What happened to Icarus?
10. Who was Perdix?
11. Why didn't Daedalus like Perdix?
12. What did Daedalus do to Perdix?
13. Who saved Perdix?

1. Mercury was the messenger of the gods.
2. He had eagles lift him and his throne into the air.
3. Yes, there were many flying creatures in ancient mythology.
4. Pegasus was the flying horse's name.
5. Yes, I think flying would be fun.
   No, I don't think flying would be fun.
6. Yes, early people were fascinated with flying.
7. He wanted to escape from prison.
8. The wings were made of feathers and wax.
9. He fell into the sea and died.
10. Perdix was the king's nephew.
11. He didn't like Perdix because Perdix was smarter than he was.
12. Daedalus pushed Perdix off a high tower.
13. The goddess Minerva saved Perdix.

Lesson 3

VOCABULARY

taffeta	contraption	experiment	lift, to
upwards	cordage	astonishing	rope
balloon	demonstration	land, to	contain, to
destroy, to	untrue		

ACTIVITY 1: Listen to the audio and your teacher read the paragraphs, then take turns reading out loud.

In 1777, a French papermaker by the name of Joseph Montgolfier was watching clothes dry over a fire. He noticed that sometimes the wet clothes were lifted up by the hot air. He wanted to find out why this happened so he started doing experiments with hot air. He believed that the smoke contained a gas, which he called "Montgolfier Gas," which could lift things.

He made a box of very thin wood, and covered it with taffeta, and set it on a table with a hole in the middle. He lit a fire under the table. The smoke went upwards through the hole, and lifted the box right off the table. Joseph became very excited and asked his brother Jacques-Étienne to come and see his experiment. He said:
"Get in a supply of taffeta and of cordage, quickly, and you will see one of the most astonishing sights in the world."

They built a much bigger contraption out of thin wood and taffeta and built a fire under it. Suddenly, it took off. Both of them held the ropes, but it pulled upwards so hard they couldn't hold it. Up, up it went, high over the buildings of Paris. Finally, the fire died down and it fell to the street. People who saw this strange, smoky thing fall on their street ran out and destroyed it. They didn't know that this was the first successful flight of a hot air balloon. That was the 14th of December, 1782.

The Montgolfier brothers could see that this experiment could be a real success, so they worked hard on a new design. At first they thought that it might not be safe for people to fly in their balloon, so they sent a sheep, a duck and a rooster on the next flight.

A huge crowd came to see the demonstration, including King Louis XVI and Marie Antoinette. The flight was very successful. The balloon went up about 500 meters and traveled about 3 kilometers.

Although the flight was a great success, and the sheep, duck and rooster landed safely, King Louis was not very happy with the demonstration. The Montgolfier brothers believed that the smoke contained the "Montgolfier Gas" so they made the fire very smoky. They threw in lots of grass and some old boots to make a lot of smoke. All of this smoke looked wonderful to the crowd, but it blew in the face of the king, and he didn't like it!

https://tinyurl.com/yrtr8n5j

Lesson 3 Continued

CONDITIONAL SENTENCES

There are three words that are used for conditional sentences:

COULD – to be able   **WOULD** - expresses intention   **SHOULD** - duty

Conditional sentences use **could** to **express doubt**,
so they are often preceded or followed by an "if" clause:

If I got home early I **could** help my mother.

Would is used to **ask politely** for something:
I **would** like coffee, please.

Should is used to **express a duty** to do something:
We **should** visit my aunt in the hospital.

CONDITIONAL SENTENCES: UNTRUE FACTS IN THE PRESENT TENSE
CLAUSE: A clause is a group of words that has a subject and a verb.

Clause 1	Clause 2
I would meet her at 7:00	if she weren't at work.

If the sentence **is untrue at the time**, use the **past tense** in the "if" clause. "**Were**" is used for both singular and plural in conditional sentences.

If I were rich, I would buy a new car
If I were a dog, I would chase cats.

ACTIVITY 2:   Divide into small groups. Ask each other the questions, then check your answers.

1. If you were there, would you fly in their balloon?
2. Would the king have liked it if there were no smoke?
3. If you could, would you fly in a balloon?
4. If you had time would you make a balloon?
5. If you had some "Montgolfier Gas", could it lift you up?
6. If you were a rooster would you like a balloon ride?
7. If you were Joseph Montgolfier would you be happy?

1. Yes, if I were there I would fly in their balloon.
   No, if I were there I wouldn't fly in their balloon.
2. Yes, he would have liked it if there were no smoke.
3. Yes, if I could I would fly in a balloon. No, if I could I wouldn't fly in a balloon.
4. Yes, if I had time I would make a balloon. No, if I had time I wouldn't make a balloon.
5. If I had some "Montgolfier Gas" it wouldn't lift me.
   There isn't a gas called "Montgolfier Gas".
6. No, if I were a rooster I wouldn't like a balloon ride.
7. Yes, if I were Joseph Montgolfier I'd be happy.

Lesson 4

VOCABULARY

kite	religious	ceremony	platform
handle	pilot	attempt, to	record, to
glider	balloon	electric	motor
helicopter	model	repair, to	hydrogen

ACTIVITY 1: Listen to the audio and your teacher read the

paragraphs, then take turns reading orally.

About 2,000 years ago the Chinese people became very good at making kites. At first they were used for religious ceremonies, then later, they flew them just for fun.

In the fifteenth century, Leonardo da Vinci made a beautiful drawing of a flying machine, that was like a helicopter. In his drawing, the pilot stood on a platform and turned a handle very quickly. This turned wings above the pilot's head and made the machine rise into the air.

People have made machines like the da Vinci drawing, but they can't make them fly. The machines were too heavy. Maybe it was just his dream.

After that, we have no records of any attempts to fly until 1799. An Englishman, Sir George Caley designed the first small model airplane. In 1804 he flew the model with a small engine. At that time, engines powerful enough to do the work were too heavy for big planes to lift.

A German, Otto Lilienthal did a lot of work with gliders. He was very interested in the flight of birds, and thought that if we had wings like birds, we could fly. In many ways, he was like a modern scientist, because he made a record of all his flights.
In fact, his records helped all of the later experimenters in flight.

Otto Lilienthal made more than 2500 flights in the gliders he made. Very little was known about flying then, and so it was dangerous work. There were many crashes, and Lilienthal had to repair his gliders many times. Unfortunately, he was killed in a crash in 1896.

While Lilienthal was working on his gliders, other people were working with balloons. With hot air or hydrogen, balloons could be lighter than air, while planes were always heavier than air. Finally, in 1884, a big balloon called La France flew around the Eiffel Tower in Paris. It had a small electric motor. It flew 8 kilometers in 23 minutes.

Because it was controlled by a motor, this is said to be the first flight made by man.

ORAL QUESTIONS TEACHER'S GUIDE

Lesson 4 Continued

ACTIVITY 2: Workbook page 8
ACTIVITY 3: Divide into small groups. Ask each other the questions,

1. Did the Chinese people make airplanes?	1. No, they made kites.
2. Did they fly in their kites?	2. No, they didn't fly in their kites.
3. Did Leonardo da Vinci's flying machine fly?	3. No, his machine didn't fly.
4. Where was Otto from?	4. Otto was from Germany.
5. Did he have motors in his flying machines?	5. No, he didn't have motors.
6. Did he make many glider flights?	6. Yes, he made many glider flights.
7. How did he help other people interested in flying?	7. He made a record of all his flights.
8. What happened to Otto?	8. He died when his glider crashed.
9. What were people using to lift their balloons?	9. People were using hot air and hydrogen to lift their balloons.
10. Were the balloons heavier than air?	10. No, the balloons were lighter than air.
11. Were the gliders heavier than air?	11. Yes, the gliders were heavier than air.
12. What was the name of the first balloon that flew around the Eiffel Tower?	12. The first balloon that flew around the Eiffel Tower was called La France.

USING CONDITIONAL SENTENCES IN THE FUTURE TENSE

If the future tense **"will"** is used, put the **"if clause" or the conditional clause**, into the **present tense**.

EXAMPLES:
I will tell him if I **see** him. He will understand if I **tell** him. I'll buy a car when I **get** there.

ACTIVITY 4: Divide into small groups. Complete the sentences,

1. I will see you when I (to get) _____ there.	1. I will see you when I get there.
2. I will cook some apples if I (to have) _____ them.	2. I will cook some apples if I have them.
3. The children will run if they (to see) _____ me.	3. The children will run if they see me.
4. You will get sick if you (to sleep, not) _____.	4. You will get sick if you don't sleep.
5. You will be late if you (to hurry, not) _____.	5. You will be late if you don't hurry.
6. I will be glad if they (to give) _____ me supper.	6. I will be glad if they give me supper.
7. I won't be able to give you any if I (to have, not) _____ any.	7. I won't be able to give you any if I don't have any.
8. I will eat supper if there (to be) _____ any.	8. I will eat supper if there is any.

EXERCISE 1: Workbook page 8 EXERCISE 2: Workbook page 9

Lesson 5

VOCABULARY

patent, to
wealthy
accident
transatlantic
scenario
reconnaissance
enemy
airline
engine
destination
Civil War
company
cabin
passenger
engineer
enormous
ocean

https://tinyurl.com/bdcsrsyv

ACTIVITY 1: Listen to the audio and your teacher read the paragraphs, then take turns reading orally.

THE ZEPPELIN

During the American Civil War, (1861 to 1865), the Union army used balloons to fly up over the enemy lines and see what they were doing. Five years later, the French used balloons in the Franco-Prussian War.

A German, Count von Zeppelin became very interested in balloons. With his friends, he designed a huge balloon. One of the people who worked with him was Gottlieb Daimler, an engineer, who later was active in working with gas engines.

The zeppelins had one or two cabins underneath the balloon for carrying people. The balloon was filled with hydrogen. The first zeppelin flight was in 1900. Count von Zeppelin patented his design in 1895.

At first there were a lot of terrible crashes. By 1908, however, their experiments were becoming very successful. In that year Count von Zeppelin formed the first airline company in the world.

Zeppelins were used a lot in the First World War. The Germans used them for reconnaissance, and some even dropped bombs.

In 1929, the "Graf Zeppelin" flew around the world!

Count Zeppelin's company built two huge zeppelins, the "Hindenburg" and the "Graf Zeppelin". These were enormous airships. The "Hindenburg" was of 245 meters long and it could carry 200 tons. After the first war, the airline company set up passenger service. They started transatlantic flights in the 1930's These were the first passengers to ever fly across an ocean.

Many of the wealthy people in the world wanted to fly across the ocean. There were regular flights from Germany to cities in North and South America.

This wonderful period in the history of flight came to a fiery ending in 1937. The Hindenburg exploded and burned while landing in New York.

ORAL QUESTIONS TEACHER'S GUIDE

Lesson 5 Continued

EXERCISES 1 and 2: Workbook page 10

ACTIVITY 2: Divide into small groups. Role play the following scenarios:
Write your conversation in a notebook, and be ready to role-play it for the class.

Scenario 1:
You are a group of young people. You have read about the zeppelins, and are talking about the early trans Atlantic flights. One of the group thinks it would be wonderful to float across the ocean in a zeppelin. One of the group thinks that it was just something that the rich people did to show their friends that they had lots of money, and that they weren't afraid. Others in the group had different ideas. Make this into a good conversation.

Scenario 2:
Your group is trying to think what it was like to go on one of the first flights across the ocean. You are talking about how fast it would go to get there in a short time – so much faster than by boat. One of your group is thinking that it would be very scary, but another is saying that it would be quite safe, because the zeppelin is over 240 meters long. Make this into a good conversation.

Scenario 3:
One of your group is saying that he/ she would like to go on a zeppelin across the ocean. It would be exciting. Another person is saying that they wouldn't like to go in a zeppelin because there might be a big wind, and it would blow the zeppelin away. Another person is saying that they think it would be too dangerous, because the zeppelin is filled with hydrogen, and it might explode. Make this into a good conversation.

Scenario 4:
In your group, one person has found that it is possible to have a ride in a hot air balloon. He / she is suggesting that if each person were to pay fifty dollars, they could all go in the balloon for an hour's ride.
One person heard that there were a couple of accidents in the United States in 2007, so they don't think it's safe. Another person likes the idea, and suggests all the things that they would see. Another person hasn't got fifty dollars, and says that even if they did have the money, they wouldn't spend it that way. Make this into a good conversation.

EXERCISE 3: Workbook page 10

The History of Flight

Intermediate to Advanced ESL Lesson plans

Student Workbook

Learning English Curriculum

Since 1999

www.efl-esl.com

Lesson 1

EXERCISE 1:
Answer the questions in complete sentences:

1. Why could Mercury travel very fast?

   _____

2. How could the emperor in Persia see all parts of his kingdom?

   _____

3. Does ancient mythology have stories about creatures that could fly?

   _____

4. What was Pegasus?

   _____

ACTIVITY 3: Divide into small groups of two or three and complete this conversation. Role-play the finished conversation several times.

Narrator You are talking with your friend about the history of flying.

: You: Have you often wished that you were a bird, and could fly through the air?

Your Friend: Yes! I would _____

You: It must be interesting to people, because there are so many stories about

flying. **Your Friend:** Yes, in Persia_____

You: There were lots of stories about flying carpets in Persia.

Your Friend:

You: _____

In the old stories, people would sit on the magic carpet, then say some magic words, and the carpet would rise into the air and take them where they wanted to go. Wouldn't that be a lot of fun?

Your Friend: I guess so, but _____

You: Well, if you don't like the thought of a magic carpet, maybe you'd like to fly on the back of Pegasus.

Your Friend: _____

You: I think you would have to wait a few hundred years, and fly in an airplane. That would be safe.

Lesson 1 Continued

EXERCISE 2: Crossword Puzzle:

ACROSS

1. its long and thin
6. goodness
7. a mythical beast
8. what birds fly with
9. the back of your foot

DOWN

1. something that means something else
2. a big bird
3. what kings and queens sit on
4. stories from the past
5. to be interested in

Lesson 2

EXERCISE 1: Answer the questions in sentences.

1. What did the king ask Daedalus to build?

2. What happened to Daedalus and Icarus after the maze was built?

3. How did Daedalus and Icarus escape?

4. What were the wings made of?

5. Why did Icarus fall into the sea?

6. Why didn't Daedalus like Perdix?

7. Why didn't Perdix die when he was pushed off the tower?

8. Why do people say that partridges don't like to fly too high?

EXERCISE 2:
Make sentences of the words below:

1. Daedalus very called who was was man smart a There.

2. fell melted sea wings, and The Icarus sun his into the.

3. father and high He to his flew listen very didn't.

4. his and hat little wings that he had was on It said heels

5. a Greeks Pegasus called had flying horse The even.

Lesson 2 Continued

EXERCISE 3:
Fill in the blanks in the following paragraph using the adjectives given below:

Daedalus and Icarus lived in _____ Greece. Daedalus worked for a _____ _____ king. This king asked Daedalus to make him a _____ maze. He wanted it to be an _____ place, so that no one could ever find their way out. When it was finished, Daedalus was a _____ man, because he was the _____ person who knew how to get out of the _____ maze. The king didn't want Daedalus to tell _____ people, so he put him and his _____ son Icarus in prison. Daedalus was _____ smart for the king. He made _____ wings for himself and Icarus. One _____ day the _____ Daedalus and Icarus flew over the _____ walls. Icarus flew too close to the _____ sun. He fell into the _____ ocean.

USE THESE WORDS:

impossible	only	warm	ancient	huge	other
young	too	sunny	deep	other	beautiful
very	rich	happy	terrible	high	wise

EXERCISE 4: Write a short paragraph telling what you'd do if you had wings and could fly:

If   I   had   wings   and   could fly_____

_____

_____

_____

_____

Helpful Phrases:

fly like the wind
fly as high as I wanted
see all the sights
go to exotic places
travel around the world
wouldn't care about anything

Lesson 2 Continued

EXERCISE 4:

MATCH THE MEANING

Write the correct meaning beside the words, using the definitions seen below:

myth _____

partridge _____

garden _____

tower _____

feather _____

escape _____

throne _____

righteousness _____

dragon _____

nephew _____

maze _____

prison _____

USE THESE WORDS:

your sister's son
a place of flowers and bushes
birds have them on their wings
a bird
a king or queen sits on it
a very high building
goodness
where they put bad people
stories from long ago
to get away
a mythical creature
a big puzzle

Lesson 3

EXERCISE 1: Answer the questions in sentences.

1. What did the Montgolfier brothers build?
   _____

2. What did they put in their first balloon?
   _____

3. Did the duck, the sheep, and the rooster fly through the air?
   _____

4. What important people watched the two brothers on their first flight?
   _____

5. Where did they get the hot air to make the balloon rise?
   _____

6. What did the brothers think caused the balloon to rise?
   _____

7. Do you think their balloon flights were dangerous?
   _____

8. The Montgolfier brothers went up in their balloon in 1783. Do people still go up in balloons?_____

EXERCISE 2: Put the word in brackets ( ) into the correct tense.

1. If I (to have) _____ a chicken, I would eat it.
2. I would ride my bicycle if I (to have) _____ it with me.
3. Maria would phone you tonight if she (to be) _____ at home.
4. You could see a movie if you (to have) _____ time.
5. If I (to be) _____ you, I wouldn't do that.
6. If you (to be) _____ rich would you be happy?
7. If I (to be) _____ king, you could be my queen.
8. If we (to have) _____ wings, we could fly.
9. If you (to see) _____ her, you would like her.
10. He would be angry if he (to be) _____ here.
11. If I (to have) _____ the money, I would buy some coffee.

Lesson 3 Continued

ACTIVITY 3: BINGO
Before playing the game the students are to write the numbers of the words in LIST 1 beside the words with the same meaning in LIST 2.

LIST 1   MATCH THE MEANING

1 prison
2 tower
3 righteousness
4 myth
5 maze
6 feather
7 partridge
8 dragon
9 nephew
10 garden
11 throne
12 escape
13 fascinate
14 snake
15 heel
16 ancient
17 symbol
18 kingdom
19 beautiful
20 messenger
21 mind
22 to heal
23 shine
24 to fly

LIST 2

WORDS TO CALL: 1 where they put bad people

to move through the air
it stands for something else
the back of your foot
a long thin creature
very pretty
he carries messages
your brother's son
very old
a king or queen sits on it
what the sun does
where the king rules
a big puzzle

to interest
stories from long ago
birds have them on their wings
a very high building
a place of flowers and bushes
you think with it
a bird
to make better
to get away
goodness
a mythical creature

		BINGO FREE		

Lesson 4

ACTIVITY 2: Divide into groups of two or three. Make a conversation about early flight.

You: I just read about the first people who really did fly through the air. It wasn't Daedalus and Icarus.

Your friend: _____ ?

You: It was the Montgolfier brothers in France. They did it for King Louis XVI and his wife Josephine.

Your friend: _____ ?

You: No, they didn't make wings, they made a balloon. They lit a fire under the balloon and it rose into the air. They thought it was the smoke that caused the balloon to rise, so they made a very smoky fire.

Your friend: _____ ?

You: No, it wasn't their first balloon, a couple of months before they put a sheep, a duck and a rooster in a balloon and made it fly.

Your friend: _____ ?

You: No, the king didn't enjoy it. The book says that the wind blew the smoke in the king's face, and he was not at all happy about it.

EXERCISE 1: Answer in sentences.

1. When were the Chinese people making kites?

   _____

2. Was Leonardo da Vinci interested in flying?

   _____

3. Did George Caley fly in his gliders?

   _____

4. Did Caley fly a model with a small engine?

   _____

5. Did Otto Lilienthal make many flights?

   _____

6. Did Lilienthal have a motor in his planes?

   _____

7. Were Lilienthal's flights dangerous?

   _____

Lesson 4 Continued

EXERCISE 2: Crossword Puzzle:

www.CrosswordWeaver.com

ACROSS

3 he flies a plane
4 a plane with no motor
10 it makes things go
11 not true
13 to fix
14 a very light gas
15 about God

DOWN

1 it goes up in the air
2 the Chinese made them long ago
5 to write down
6 very surprising
7 you turn it
8 a small copy of something
9 wreck
12 towards the sky

Lesson 5

EXERCISE 1: Make correct sentences of the following words:

1. the, time, will, to, have, go, if, I, I, library
   _____

2. phone, am, you, late, will, If, I, I
   _____

3. London, money, I, had, I, fly, enough, if, would, to
   _____

4. I, I, if, him, would, him, tell, saw
   _____

5. see, ask, will, her, I, if, I, her
   _____

6. were, He, if, wouldn't, alone, there, he, go
   _____

7. early, car, I, I, the, If, home, wash, get, could
   _____

8. high, If, I, wouldn't, were, so, Icarus, I, fly
   _____

EXERCISE 2: Answer the questions in sentences.

1. Were Zeppelins the first flying machines to carry passengers?
   _____

2. Who had the first patent on Zeppelins?
   _____

3. Did Zeppelins ever carry passengers across the Atlantic Ocean?
   _____

4. Were Zeppelins used during the First World War?
   _____

5. Who started the first airline company in the world?
   _____

Lesson 5 Continued

EXERCISE 3:

MATCH THE MEANING
Write the correct meaning beside the words, using the definitions seen below:

wealthy _____

transatlantic _____

scenario _____

reconnaissance _____

enemy _____

airline _____

destination _____

enormous _____

accident _____

to attempt _____

glider _____

hydrogen _____

USE THESE WORDS:

very large
crosses the Atlantic ocean
where you are going
person or people against you
a company that has airplanes
something bad that happens
possible situation
a plane with no motor
to try
exploration for information
a very light gas
have a lot of money

The History of Flight

Intermediate to Advanced ESL Lesson plans

Teacher Guide

Learning English
Curriculum
Since 1999
www.efl-esl.com

Lesson 1

ORAL QUESTIONS

Are people still fascinated with the sky? Who was Mercury said to be? Why could he travel quickly? How did the emperor of Persia travel through the air?

Yes, they are still fascinated with the sky. He was said to be messenger of the gods. He had wings on his feet and hat.

He sat on his throne and eagles lifted him into the air.

Who had a symbol of a winged sun?

The ancient Egyptians had a symbol of a winged sun.
The Greeks believed in Pegasus.

Who believed in Pegasus?
Were there flying creatures in ancient mythology?

Yes, there were flying creatures in ancient mythology.

EXERCISE 1:

1. Why could Mercury travel very fast?
   He had wings on his feet and hat.
2. How could the emperor in Persia see all parts of his kingdom? *He had eagles come and lift him into the air.*
3. Does ancient mythology have stories about creatures that could fly? *Yes, ancient mythology has stories about creatures that could fly*
4. What was Pegasus?
   It was a flying horse.

EXERCISE 2: Crossword Puzzle solution.

Lesson 2

ORAL QUESTIONS

Where did Daedalus and Icarus live?	They lived in Greece.
What did they want to do?	They wanted to fly.
Why did they want to fly.	They wanted to escape from prison. He made them from wax and feathers.
What did Daedalus make the wings from?	
What did Daedalus tell Icarus before they flew?	He told him not to fly too high.
Did Icarus listen to his father?	No, he didn't listen to his father.
What happened to Icarus?	He flew too high and his wings melted.
How did Icarus die?	He fell into the sea.
Who was Perdix?	Perdix was Daedalus' nephew.
Was Perdix smart?	Yes, Perdix was very smart.
What did Daedalus do to Perdix?	He pushed him off a high tower.
Did Perdix die from the fall?	No, he was changed into a partridge,
Who saved him?	The goddess Minerva saved him.

EXERCISE 1:

1. What did the king ask Daedalus to build?
   He asked him to build a maze.
2. What happened to Daedalus and Icarus after the maze was built?
   They were put in prison.
3. How did Daedalus and Icarus escape?
   Icarus made wings and they flew out.
4. What were the wings made of?
   They were made of feathers and wax.
5. Why did Icarus fall into the sea?
   He flew too close to the sun and his wings melted.
6. Why didn't Daedalus like Perdix?
   Perdix was smarter than him.
7. Why didn't Perdix die when he was pushed off the tower?
   Minerva changed him into a partridge.
8. Why do people say that partridges don't like to fly too high?
   They say that they still remember falling off the tower.

EXERCISE 2:

1. Daedalus very called who was was man smart a There.
   There was a man called Daedalus who was very smart.
2. fell melted sea wings, and The Icarus sun his into the.
   The sun melted his wings and Icarus fell into the sea.
3. father and high He to his flew listen very didn't.
   He didn't listen to his father and flew very high.
4. his and hat little wings that he had was on It said heels
   It was said that he had little wings on his hat and heels.
5. a Greeks Pegasus called had flying horse The even.
   The Greeks even had a flying horse called Pegasus.

Lesson 2 Continued

6. himself, feathers wax made wings for using two and big He.
   He made two big wings for himself using wax and feathers.
7. pushed Daedalus a high day, Perdix tower One off.
   One day, Daedalus pusher Perdix off a high tower.

EXERCISE 3:

Daedalus and Icarus lived in **ancient** Greece. Daedalus worked for a **very rich** king. This king asked Daedalus to make him a **beautiful** maze. He wanted it to be an **impossible** place, so that no one could ever find their way out. When it was finished, Daedalus was a **wise** man, because he was the **only** person who knew how to get out of the **terrible** maze. The king didn't want Daedalus to tell **other** people, so he put him and his **young** son Icarus in prison. Daedalus was **too** smart for the king. He made **huge** wings for himself and Icarus. One **sunny** day the **happy** Daedalus and Icarus flew over the **high** walls.

Icarus flew too close to the **warm** sun. He fell into the **deep** ocean.

EXERCISE 4:

MATCH THE MEANING

myth	*stories from long ago*	partridge	*a bird*
garden	*a place of flowers and bushes*	tower	*a very high building*
feather	*birds have them on their wings*	escape	*to get away*
throne	*a king or queen sits on it*	righteousness	*goodness*
dragon	*a mythical creature*	nephew	*your sister's son*
maze	*a big puzzle*	prison	*where they put bad people*

Lesson 3

ORAL QUESTIONS

Did Montgolfier gas make the balloons rise?
No, it was hot air that made them rise.

What happened to their first balloon?
People destroyed it.

What did they make their balloons of?
They made them of thin wood and taffeta.

Why did they send the sheep, duck and rooster up in the first flight?
They didn't know if it would be safe for humans to fly in the balloon.

Lesson 3 Continued

On the flight before the king, did the balloon go up very high?
Yes, it went up about 500 meters.

Why did the brothers make the fire in the balloon very smoky?
They thought the smoke lifted the balloon.

Did the sheep, the duck and the rooster survive the flight?
Yes, they survived the flight.

Did many people see the first flight?
Yes, a huge crowd came to see it.

Did King Louis enjoy seeing the first flight? Why didn't he enjoy it?
No, he didn't enjoy it.
He didn't like all the smoke.

EXERCISE 1:
1. What did the Montgolfier brothers build?
   They built a balloon.
2. What did they put in their first balloon?
   They put a duck, a sheep, and a rooster in the first balloon.
3. Did the duck, the sheep, and the rooster fly through the air?
   Yes, the duck, the sheep, and the rooster flew through the air.
4. What important people watched the two brothers on their first flight?
   The king and his wife watched the first flight.
5. Where did they get the hot air to make the balloon rise?
   They got the hot air from a fire.
6. What did the brothers think caused the balloon to rise?
   They thought the smoke caused it to rise.
7. Do you think their balloon flights were dangerous?
   Yes, I think they were dangerous.
8. The Montgolfier brothers went up in their balloon in 1783.
   Do people still go up in balloons?
   Yes, people still go up in balloons.

EXERCISE 2:   Put the word in brackets ( ) into the correct tense.

1. If I **had** a chicken, I would eat it.
2. I would ride my bicycle if I **had** it with me.
3. Maria would phone you tonight if she **were** at home.
4. You could see a movie if you **had** time.
5. If I **were** you, I wouldn't do that.
6. If you **were** rich would you be happy?
7. If I **were** king, you could be my queen.
8. If we **had** wings, we could fly.
9. If you **saw** her, you would like her.
10. He would be angry if he **were** here.
11. If I **had** the money, I would buy some coffee.

Lesson 3 Continued

ACTIVITY 3:   **BINGO**

1. prison — *where they put bad people*
2. tower — *a very high building*
3. righteousness — *goodness*
4. myth — *stories from long ago*
5. maze — *a big puzzle*
6. feather — *birds have them on their wings*
7. partridge — *a bird*
8. dragon — *a mythical creature*
9. nephew — *your brother's son*
10. garden — *a place of flowers and bushes*
11. throne — *a king or queen sits on it*
12. escape — *to get away*
13. fascinate — *to interest*
14. snake — *a long thin creature the*
15. heel — *back of your foot*
16. ancient — *very old*
17. symbol — *it stands for something else*
18. kingdom — *where the king rules*
19. beautiful — *very pretty*
20. messenger — *he carries messages*
21. mind — *you think with it*
22. to heal — *to make better*
23. shine — *what the sun does*
24. to fly — *to move through the air*

Lesson 4

ORAL QUESTIONS

Would you be happy if you were a hero?
Yes, I'd be happy if I were a hero.
No, I wouldn't be happy if I were a hero.

Where would you live if you had a lot of money?
I'd live in _____ if I had a lot of money.

Would you fly in a balloon if you could?
Yes, I'd fly in a balloon if I could.
No, I wouldn't fly in a balloon if I could.

If you had time would you travel.
Yes, I'd travel if I had time.
No, I wouldn't travel if I had time.

If you were hungry would you go to a restaurant?
Yes, if I were hungry, I'd go to a restaurant.
No, if I were hungry, I wouldn't go to a restaurant.

If you had an apple would you eat it?
Yes, if I had an apple I'd eat it.
No, if I had an apple I wouldn't eat it.

Would you visit your friends if they were sick?
Yes, I'd visit my friends if they were sick.
No, I wouldn't visit my friends if they were sick.

If you are tired will you go to bed early?
Yes, if I'm tired I'll go to bed early.
No, if I'm tired I won't go to bed early.

If you had a horse would you ride it?
Yes, if I had a horse I'd ride it.
No, if I had a horse I wouldn't ride it.

Will you have a holiday this summer if you have time?
Yes, I'll have a holiday if I have time.
No, I won't have a holiday if I have time.

Lesson 4 Continued

ACTIVITY 2: *POSSIBLE ANSWERS.*

You: I just read about the first people who really did fly through the air. It wasn't Daedalus and Icarus.

Your friend: *Who was it?*

You: It was the Montgolfier brothers in France. They did it for King Louis XVI and his wife Josephine.

Your friend: *How did they do it? Did they make wings?*

You: No, they didn't make wings, they made a balloon. They lit a fire under the balloon and it rose into the air. They thought it was the smoke that caused the balloon to rise, so they made a very smoky fire.

Your friend: *Was it their first balloon?*

You: No, it wasn't their first balloon, a couple of months before they put a sheep, a duck and a rooster in a balloon and made it fly.

Your friend: *Did the king like it?*

You: No, the king didn't enjoy it. The book says that the wind blew the smoke in the king's face, and he was not at all happy about it.

EXERCISE 1: Answer in sentences.

1. When were the Chinese people making kites?
   They were making them 2000 years ago.
2. Was Leonardo da Vinci interested in flying?
   Yes, he was interested in flying.
3. Did George Caley fly in his gliders?
   No, his gliders were only small models.
4. Did Caley fly a model with a small engine?
   Yes, he flew a model with a small engine.
5. Did Otto Lilienthal make many flights?
   Yes, he made more than 2500 flights.
6. Did Lilienthal have a motor in his planes? *No, his planes were all gliders.*
7. Were Lilienthal's flights dangerous?
   Yes, they were dangerous.
8. Why did Lilienthal stop flying?
   He was killed when one of his gliders crashed.

**EXERCISE 2:
Crossword Puzzle solution:**

Lesson 5

ORAL QUESTIONS

If there were Zeppelins today would you fly across the Atlantic in one?
Yes, I'd fly across the Atlantic in one.

Would you like to fly a kite?
Yes, I'd like to fly a kite.
No, I wouldn't like to fly a kite.

The first people to fly used gliders, didn't they?
Yes, they did.

Was Leonardo da Vinci interested in flying?
Yes, he was interested in flying.

What did Otto Lilienthal do?
He made many flights with gliders.

What happened to him?
He died in a crash.

When was the first flight with a motor?
It was in 1884.

What kind of flying machine made the first flight?
It was a balloon with an electric motor.

Where did it fly?
It flew around the Eiffel Tower in Paris.

Do we see Zeppelins flying today?
Yes, we sometimes see Zeppelins flying today.
No, we don't see them flying today.

Would you fly to another country if you had the money?
Yes, I'd fly to another country if I had the money.
No, I wouldn't fly to another country if I had the money.

EXERCISE 1:

1. the, time, will, to, have, go, if, I, I, library
   I will go to the library if I have time.
2. phone, am, you, late, will, If, I, I
   If I am late I will phone you.
3. London, money, I, had, I, fly, enough, if, would, to
   I would fly to London if I had enough money.
4. I, I, if, him, would, him, tell, saw
   I would tell him if I saw him
5. see, ask, will, her, I, if, I, her
   I will ask her if I see her.
6. were, He, if, wouldn't, alone, there, he, go
   He wouldn't go there if he were alone.
7. early, car, I, I, the, If, home, wash, get, could
   If I get home early I could wash the car.
8. high, If, I, wouldn't, were, so, Icarus, I, fly
   If I were Icarus I wouldn't fly so high.

Activity 2 Student Reader:

Scenario 1: Suggest to the group what a new thing flying must have been.
Scenario 2: Suggest that it would be wonderful for people who get sea sick in boats.
Scenario 3: Suggest that it would likely be safer to go by boat, but the Zeppelin would be exciting.

Scenario 4: Point out that although it would be very exciting, it might also be very dangerous.

Lesson 5 Continued

EXERCISE 2:

1. Were Zeppelins the first flying machines to carry passengers?
   Yes, Zeppelins were the first flying machines to carry passengers.
2. Who had the first patent on Zeppelins?
   Count von Zeppelin had the first patent.
3. Did Zeppelins ever carry passengers across the Atlantic Ocean?
   Yes, they carried many passengers across the Atlantic Ocean.
4. Were Zeppelins used during the First World War?
   Yes, Zeppelins were used during the First World War.
5. Who started the first airline company in the world?
   Count von Zeppelin started the first airline company.

EXERCISE 3:

MATCH THE MEANING

wealthy	*have a lot of money*	transatlantic	*crosses the Atlantic ocean*
scenario	*possible situation*	reconnaissance	*exploration for information*
enemy	*person or people against*	airline	*a company that has airplanes*
destination	*you where you are going*	enormous	*very large*
accident	*something bad that happens*	to attempt	*to try*
glider	*a plane with no motor*	hydrogen	*a very light gas*

Visit us Online for More

https://www.efl-esl.com

BEGINNERS LESSON PLANS BOOK 1

20 complete lesson plans
3 Textbooks plus
Downloadable Audio and Video

Includes:

- Student Reader
- Student Workbook
- Teachers Guide
- 20 lessons
- 5 tests
- 4 reviews
- Glossary
- Download PDF or Paperback

Book 1 Overview

BEGINNERS LESSON PLANS BOOK 2

20 complete lesson plans
3 Textbooks plus
Downloadable Audio and Video

Includes:

- Student Reader
- Student Workbook
- Teachers Guide
- 20 lessons
- 5 tests
- 4 reviews
- Glossary
- Download PDF or Paperback

Book 2 Overview

Teach Your Students Online

You provide the Students
We provide the curriculum and platform

- Level 1 Beginners – Book 1 now available
- Teachers – FREE
- Students – $19.99/month
- Our commission – 30%
- Fully Customizable

https://teacher.efl-esl.com

Online ESL Teaching Platforms – The Complete Guide

Learn:

- Challenges of online teaching
- Certification Options
- What to look for in an online ESL teaching platform
- Tips for online promotion

https://efl-esl.com/teach-your-students-online/

High Beginners ESL Book 1

includes 3 Textbooks plus video and audio

- Full Audio and Video
- Complete Lesson Plans ready for the classroom
- Student Reader
- Student Workbook
- Teachers Guide
- 20 lessons
- 5 tests
- 4 reviews
- Glossary
- Download PDF or paperback

Book 1 Overview

High Beginners ESL Book 2

includes 3 Textbooks plus video and audio

- Full audio and video
- Student Reader
- Student Workbook
- Teacher's Guide
- 20 lessons
- 5 tests
- 2 review lessons
- Glossary
- PDF Format Download
- Download PDF or Paperback

Book 2 Overview

Beginners ESL Video Workbook

innovative ESL Video Workbook designed especially for beginners learning English as a second language! This comprehensive toolkit integrates:

Interactive Videos: Engaging videos presenting fundamental English concepts, ensuring users not only listen and understand but also speak and practice in real-time.

Enriching Audio: Complementary audio materials that reinforce lesson topics, enhance pronunciation, and improve listening skills.

Exercises & Activities: A variety of exercises including:

  • **Role Plays:** Develop conversational skills through real-life scenarios.
  • **Match the Meaning:** Connect words with their respective meanings to build vocabulary.
  • **Fill in the Blank:** Improve grammar and context understanding by completing sentences.
  • **Question and Answer:** Boost comprehension through interactive Q&A sessions.

Learn More https://efl-esl.com/video-workbooks/

Listening and Speaking Workbook

Complete Listening and Speaking English Workbook – includes full downloadable audio!

- Vocabulary for each Lesson
- Everyday Conversations – Listen to full audio then role-play!
- 14 Lessons
- 2 Review Chapters
- 2 Full Audio Tests with Answer Key
- Role Play
- Telephone Conversations and role play
- Question and Answer Dialogues

https://efl-esl.com/listening-speaking-english/

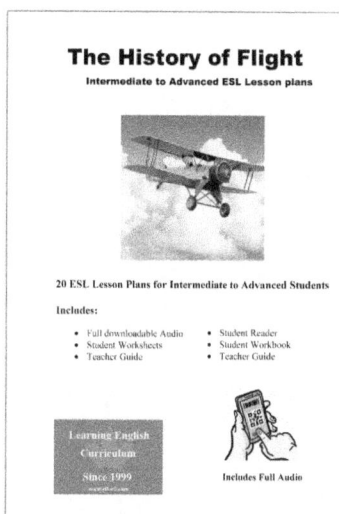

Intermediate to Advanced ESL Lesson Plans for Adults
From the Ancient Greeks to Leonardo Da Vinci's flying machines, to Orville and Wilbur Wright, to WWII flying Ace, the Red Baron, to modern day space travel!

Includes:

- **Full audio**
- 20 Lessons – 40 hours of classroom time!
- Print as many Copies as Required!
- Teacher's guide
- Student Reader
- Student Workbook
- Complete instructions — ready for the classroom
- No preparation

https://efl-esl.com/curriculum/flight/

Children's ESL

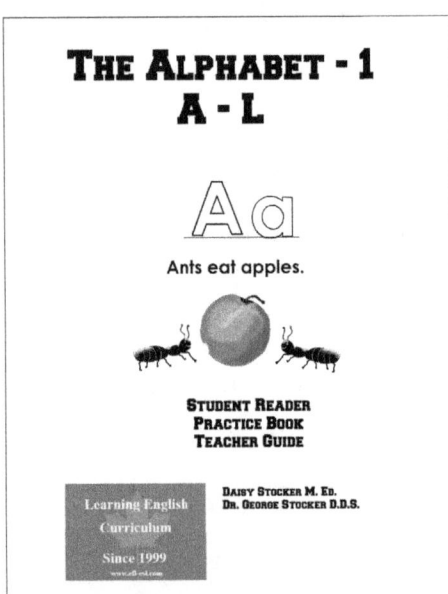

This book introduces the alphabet from A to L and the numbers from 1 – 10.

Includes:

- Student book – 37 pages
- Student Workbook – 24 pages
- Teacher's Guide Book – 50 pages
- Glossary — 142 new words
- Colorful games and activities suitable for lamination –use over and over!

https://efl-esl.com/alphabet-activities-for-esl-students/

ESL Graphic Novels for Kids (Comic Books)

These books offer an oral approach for young ESL / EFL students aged 6 - 10.

They contain high interest stories, written in the graphics novel format that children love. This is very suitable for supplementary study, home school, as well as for summer camps.

https://efl-esl.com/esl-graphic-novels-for-children/

www.ingramcontent.com/pod-product-compliance
Lightning Source LLC
Chambersburg PA
CBHW080734230426
43665CB00020B/2732